FINANCIAL
ADVISOR'S
7 STEPS TO VIDEO
MARKETING SUCCESS

JILL ADDISON

Jill Addison, Inc.

PO Box 1222

Spring Valley, CA 91979

Info@FinancialAdvisorNewClientMachine.com

ISBN-13: 978-1519164865

This publication is designed to provide accurate and authoritative
information in regard to the subject matter covered. It is sold with the
understanding that the author and publisher are not engaged in rendering
legal, accounting, or other professional services. The author and publisher
shall not be liable for your misuse of this material and shall have neither
liability nor responsibility to anyone with respect to any loss or damage
caused, or alleged to be caused, directly or indirectly by the information
contained in this book. The author and/or publisher do not guarantee that
anyone following these techniques, suggestions, tips, ideas or strategies will
become successful. If legal advice or other expert assistance is required, the
services of a competent professional person should be sought.

This book is dedicated to financial advisors like you who want to make the world a better place by helping your clients live their dreams through your invaluable financial planning services.

Table of Contents

About the Author

Jill Addison is an Internet Marketing Expert & Video Specialist for Financial Advisors who has helped hundreds of small business owners and financial advisors like you generate hundreds of thousands of dollars in new business by leveraging cutting edge video marketing strategies (powered by YouTube, Social Media and Email Marketing) to grow your practice quickly.

Her 10 years of experience in the video production world and her fascination with finance converged in the creation of video strategies and systems to help financial advisors move their marketing onto the internet as quickly and easily as possible.

She has successfully worked with compliance departments at LPL Financial, Guardian Life Insurance Company of America, and Wells Fargo Advisors to create entertaining and educational video content that attracts ideal clients and positions financial advisors like you with authority, credibility, and local star power.

Jill has always been a firm believer in the power of the media to reach the masses with messages that matter. Her credits include a feature film that has been translated into more than 100 languages and seen by millions of people around the world, as well as infomercials that have generated millions of dollars in sales, short films that have inspired charitable giving, and hundreds of promotional videos that have grown small businesses around the United States and Canada.

Forward by Amy McIlwain

I've known Jill for several years now and have always been impressed with her innovative video solutions for financial advisors. As the founder of Financial Social Media, I'm passionate about helping advisors move their marketing onto the internet, and video is definitely a huge piece.

Jill's book helps make video marketing simple and easy for financial advisors. After reading this book, you'll understand why and how video marketing works to attract your ideal client in an effortless way, and you'll have the tools you need to make it happen. Jill has a great way of explaining things that makes it easy for even a beginner to understand, while also helping advanced marketers take it to the next level.

I've used the techniques Jill describes in this book, and they've literally made me a celebrity. They can do the same thing for you.

Devote a little time in the next week or two to read and absorb this game-changing content, because it can transform your business like it's transformed mine.

Stay Social!
Amy McIlwain

Amy McIlwain's Achievements Include:

- **Author** of the Best-Selling book: *The Social Advisor: Social Media Secrets of the Financial Industry*

- **Founder** of Financial Social Media, a company dedicated to helping financial advisors navigate compliance issues surrounding social media

- **International Speaker**

- Digital & Social Media Marketing **Expert** with focus on Financial & Insurance Compliance

- Appeared on **FOX, CBS, ABC, NBC**

Free Bonus with This Book

As the owner of this book, you are entitled to a free 60-minute Online Video Training Seminar (Value: $295) with Jill Addison.

To claim your spot, visit: www.FAVideoTraining.com

In this Online Video Training Seminar, I personally walk you through the best techniques and strategies to maximize the power of online video to grow your financial advisory practice.

You'll hear case studies you can't hear anywhere else, and glean valuable insights for how to replicate those successes in your own business.

You'll Learn:

- How to make people pre-disposed to become your client before you ever meet with them

- How to motivate your clients to refer you to new clients on a regular basis

- How to make your clients LOVE you even more and naturally refer you at a faster and faster rate

- 3 keys to keep your current clients happy

- How to create an online presence that moves people several steps along in your sales process before you ever even talk with them in person

- How to build authority, credibility and celebrity with your video content

- One sneaky little trick that will make it impossible for your clients NOT to refer you

- The one single thing that will make the difference between them referring you or not referring you

- A covert ops way to get testimonial-type credibility that your compliance department will not blink an eye at

- How to strategically get 5-7 bounces out of each video

- How video accelerates every other marketing strategy you have, so it's not just one tool, it's like a super tool that makes every other tool more effective

- How to take your current real life relationships onto the internet, and also how to take your internet relationships into real life relationships

- WHY video is working so well, in case you're one of the few who are still skeptical about video

- Our story of how video helps us get calls from people we don't even know, who were referred by people we don't even know, all because of our videos

- And More

This Online Video Training Seminar is free for you as the owner of this book, but be sure to claim your spot right away, since we're not sure how long this training will be available at the link below.

Visit www.FAVideoTraining.com today to get access to your FREE Bonus 60-Minute Online Video Training Seminar.

"I'm at a point in my practice where I only work with people I like. I want to work with people who are truly interested in becoming a partner in my success, and the value and values Jill and her company bring to the table match up very well with where I want to go with my practice."

Todd Anderson
Managing Partner at Anderson Financial Group

"What I want to tell Financial Advisors is, you know you need video. You've seen the power of it, there's something magical about it. So just get out there and do it!"

Joe Simonds
Digital Marketing Maverick
Creator of "Advisor Black Box"

"Jill is AWESOME!! Jill was professional, easy to access, gave excellent guidance and the value for money was amazing. I should know I'm The Money Finder!"

Stephanie Holmes-Winton
Financial Services Speaker at "The Money Finder"

"The #1 thing you need to do today in your financial services practice is to create engaging, educational content for your marketing, like videos."

Marty Morua
Technology Advisor for RIAs at Allbackoffice Consulting, LLC

"Jill did my video and is the best there is in the video world!"

Dave Elhoff
Financial Advisor
San Diego, CA

"Every part of this content spoke to me. Jill knows our industry and that most of us are behind the curve on digital marketing. The content made perfect sense to me and helped me get up and running very quickly with video marketing strategies."

Ernest Almanza
Financial Advisor
Dallas/Ft. Worth Area

Acknowledgements

It's my pleasure to publicly thank and recognize the people who made this book possible.

First, I want to thank my husband, Eric Addison, owner of www.100AcreFilms.com. After watching Eric run his own video production business, I thought, "I bet I could do that," so I gave it a try. Eric supported me and believed in me, he gave me his leftover video equipment to launch my business, and he even came with me on my first few video shoots to help me get my business off the ground. Thank you for this, and so much more, my love.

I also want to thank my Dad, who was the model of business success for me growing up. He achieved much more than he ever even thought he could as a business owner, and I'm grateful he shared what he learned in his journey with me. I miss you, Dad. (My dad passed away in 2013.)

Thank you to Henry Evans, Author of The Hour a Day Entrepreneur and my business coach. You, more than anyone else, are responsible for this book coming into being. Thank you for pushing me, guiding me, and encouraging me along the path to entrepreneurial success.

Thanks also to Robert Kiyosaki, Author of Rich Dad Poor Dad. This book was instrumental in igniting a desire in me to move from being an employee to an entrepreneur.

And last but most importantly, thank you God for all You are and for all that will be.

Chapter 1

What You'll Learn in This Book

In this book, you're going to learn about some exciting video and internet marketing trends, ideas and case studies that you can't hear anywhere else.

If you are a financial advisor who wants to help more people with your expertise and get certainty about where your next client is coming from, then you are in the right place.

In this book, you will learn:

How you can help more people with your expertise and get certainty about where your next client is coming from

- How other financial advisors are already using these new marketing tactics on the internet and seeing exciting results

- How to keep the clients you already have and make them love you even more

- How to get new referrals from your current clients in a way that's comfortable and enjoyable for both you and them

- How to leverage internet marketing strategies to multiply your results

If these are things you want to know, you're in the right place.

I've been working with financial professionals and other professional service providers since 2009, helping people like you get new clients with new online marketing strategies like video.

What I've noticed is that it seems like a lot of financial advisors are just hoping to survive on referrals. And referrals are wonderful, they're some of the easiest business to close, which is why it's tempting to only focus on getting more referrals. But the most dangerous number in business is the number one. When you just have one big client, or one key employee, or one product you sell, or one strategy to get new clients, that's a dangerous place to be. For instance, I know a financial professional who relied on only referrals for years, and then one day the economy took a dump and suddenly all his new business just dried up overnight. He had not properly prepared for that kind of risk. He had not invested in any other strategies to generate clients. So he was at the mercy of other people to send him referrals. And when the referrals just stopped coming, those were some scary and really hard months for him, because he only had one strategy for getting new clients. He was putting all his eggs in the referral basket.

And he's not alone. More and more financial advisors are leaving the business every year because they just can't find enough clients. According to the Christian Science Monitor, 7,000 financial advisors threw in the towel last year alone, and that downward trend is expected to continue with 19,000 more financial advisors giving up their practices in the next five years. (source: http://www.csmonitor.com/Business/The-Reformed-Broker/2012/0810/Want-to-be-a-financial-adviser-Read-this-first)

But I want to make sure you don't end up like that. I want to help you ramp things up so that you're not one of those statistics. So I've created some great tools, systems and strategies for you to get new clients. We're going to dive into those over the next couple hours it takes you to read this book.

I recommend that you treat this book as part business book and part training manual. Refer to it often for practical tips on how to maximize the effectiveness of your videos, and use it as a delegation tool to assign the strategies we'll be talking about to your assistant or your team.

Inside this book you'll find step-by-step instructions for how to implement each of the strategies you'll be learning, including screenshots and video tutorial links to help you see exactly how to implement these ideas.

Why This is Important To You Now

Have you ever said any of these things?

- "**Seminars** aren't working like they used to, I know I need a new marketing strategy."

- "**Referrals** are the best kind of lead, but there are never enough of them to really take my practice all the way to where I want to go."

- "I really don't want to do all this **marketing** work, I just want more clients."

- "I just want to **help more people** with their financial planning."

- "**I wish I knew** where my next client was coming from and when."

- "I know **marketing on the internet** is the direction things are going, but I don't know how to do it."

I wrote this book to solve all these problems for you, because financial advisors who don't keep up with where marketing is going these days will be put out of business in the next 3-5 years.

I've worked with enough financial advisors that I have a pretty good idea of what may be going through your mind right now about why you're afraid this might not work for you. So let's just address those questions up front.

1. **What about compliance?** I know this is a tough part of doing marketing as a financial advisor. Every job has its pros and

cons, and for financial advisors, marketing is a little more difficult because of compliance regulations. The good news is, we have successfully worked with compliance departments at LPL Financial, Wells Fargo Advisors and Guardian Life Insurance Company of America to get our video content approved and into use for many advisors like you, so it can be done. This means that compliance is not a barrier to using these video strategies to grow your practice.

2. **Will this really work for me?** I'm going to be sharing some case studies of how these video strategies have helped other financial advisors make hundreds of thousands of dollars by capturing new clients on the internet. If it can work for other financial advisors, it can work for you.

3. **Do I have to do other internet marketing strategies besides video to make this work?** Yes. These video marketing strategies are for financial advisors who are committed to taking their marketing online and want to accelerate their results and go all in. So if that's not you, these video marketing strategies are not for you.

But if you want to get the same results that other financial advisors are getting with internet marketing and you're willing to commit to internet marketing and really go all in, then here's what you can expect.

In this book, you're going to learn exactly how to use internet marketing to get your practice to where you really want it to be, so you can get the satisfaction of helping more people and being successful, whatever that means to you. Maybe it means more time and money to travel, more time with family, or more security about your own retirement. When you master marketing for your business, especially internet marketing, all these doors will swing open for you.

So to start off, let me tell you about my story with internet marketing.

Chapter 2

Jill's Story

When I moved to San Diego in 2009, I started a new business at the same time. I thought, "How will anyone ever remember me or know me?" San Diego was the biggest city I'd ever lived in, and moving here felt like going to college all over again. I felt lost in a sea of strangers. I was meeting tons of people at networking groups, but never seeing them again.

But I started learning some marketing techniques that seemed like the most important next steps for me to take to actually grow my business. I remember thinking, "How will any of this marketing on the internet result in lasting relationships? How can what I do on the internet actually result in real relationships with real people? I feel like it just goes into a big black hole, like it doesn't make any difference. How do you do this and make it work?"

But I had learned a few marketing tips, just a handful of things that seemed like the most important things to do next in my marketing. So, even though I didn't know what would happen as a result, I started putting those things into practice. One of those marketing strategies was using videos in my email marketing. So I started doing a 1-Minute Video Marketing Tip of the Month. (If you're not already getting my 1-Minute Tips, you can sign up at www.JillAddison.com.) I started providing valuable information and content about things I knew the people on my email list cared about. I knew it would be helpful to them. So, I started helping them on the internet, every month, with these 1-Minute Video Tips.

And I couldn't believe what happened.

It didn't happen overnight, but as I was consistent about this marketing strategy I started to see some mind-blowing results.

And by the way, consistency is the #1 thing that makes marketing work; no marketing will work without that critical ingredient: consistency.

But back to my tips…what happened was that my Video Tips made me famous. People told me, "You're everywhere!" and "I feel like I see you all the time," even though I hadn't seen them in months, sometimes years.

It kept me top of mind and gave me celebrity status.

One big reason why it worked so well is because no one else was doing video tips. So I had that "first to market" advantage. And that advantage is available to you today as a financial advisor, by the way. How many financial advisors do you know who already have a video strategy in place to bring them new clients and referrals on a regular basis?

Now I get referrals regularly from people I don't even know because of my online presence and videos. They feel like they know me and they trust me because I show my expertise through the content of my videos. And they see me online consistently, with video content that's helpful to them. It's built my credibility, my authority, my celebrity, and most importantly my referability. And it can do the same thing for you.

Another amazing result of using videos consistently is that my website went from being totally lost and invisible on the internet to being on Google Page 1. Now people call me because they're searching on the internet for services that I can provide, and they find me because of all the videos on my website. We'll go into this strategy more deeply a little later in this book.

So the bottom line is, my video marketing on the internet elevated me from being lost and invisible on the internet to being an authority that people trust and can comfortably refer to others, even when they don't even know me personally. That's what an online presence with video can do for you too.

So, let's jump into *how* that can work for you by looking at how it's worked for other financial advisors.

Chapter 3

Case Studies You Won't Hear Anywhere Else

Kevin's Story

Kevin is a financial advisor in Atlanta, Georgia. When Kevin posted one of the whiteboard videos we made for him on Facebook, a friend of his from high school that he was connected to on Facebook said, "Kevin, are you a financial advisor? We need to talk to you." So this was a very hot lead, it was someone that already knew Kevin, trusted him, and liked him, she just didn't realize how he could help her.

Figure 3.1 Kevin, a financial advisor in Atlanta, gained a new client worth approximately $200,000.00 through just one Facebook post.

Since this Facebook post, Suzanne has become Kevin's client and that one engagement was worth over $200,000.00. That's a 2,400% ROI on his video investment.

THAT ONE CLIENT IS WORTH OVER $200,000.00.

A 2400% ROI

To watch an example of the kind of whiteboard video Kevin used to get these fantastic results, visit my YouTube Playlist for financial advisors here: www.bit.do/FAPlaylist You may browse our library of 40 1-minute whiteboard animated videos from our Turnkey Video Library at this link.

Alicia's Story

Another one of my clients, Alicia, has gotten amazing results from the whiteboard videos we created for her law practice.

Here's one story: one of her clients runs a payroll company. He saw her video on social media and shared it. That triggered comments and questions from his clients which led to him hiring her for more services. Her video created new business for her, just from posting it on Facebook. See how this spreads online? Her return on investment from just that one client and one video was at least 10 times what she invested in her whole series of videos.

Alicia also told me that her click-through rate for video content is five times higher than links to articles. People want to watch video. So she's planning to start incorporating video into all her weekly newsletters.

She noticed that more people were engaging with her content on her blog and social media when she posted videos. They were making comments, asking questions, and even emailing her and calling her with questions generated from the videos.

Here's one last way she uses her videos: when people reach out for a consultation, she emails them a video related to their concern before the consultation. This positions her as an expert and triggers deeper thinking so she and her prospective client can talk more seriously about engagement. So not only have her videos helped her get new business through people engaging online with her videos, they also help speed up her new client intake process.

Wouldn't you like to have these kinds of results?

ALICIA'S STORY

Figure 3.2 Alicia, an attorney in San Diego, got an ROI of ten times her initial video investment from just one Facebook post. Her videos consistently generate a click-through rate five times higher than text or photos; her videos also generate comments, questions, emails and phone calls. Alicia's videos help her engage with prospective clients on the internet better than any other marketing tool.

Chapter 4

Why Whiteboard Videos Work

Here's why these whiteboard videos work:

1. Dopamine

When people see images being drawn in whiteboard videos, at the moment they realize what's being drawn, they experience a burst of dopamine, the chemical in our brains associated with delight at something unexpected. These videos actually make people happy. And when you've put your prospective client in a happy state of mind, they're much more likely to take the next step toward becoming your client.

If you're not sure what whiteboard videos are, visit this link to watch some examples: www.bit.do/FAPlaylist

People make buying decisions based on emotion, then justify them later with logic. So when you provide a pleasurable emotional experience for your prospective clients, you prime them to like you and want to trust you, which leads to a higher likelihood of them becoming your client.

2. Make Complex Concepts Simple

Whiteboard videos are especially well-suited for financial information, because they help make complex concepts simple. I have actually had the experience where I helped a client write a script, and then sent it off to my animators, and when I saw the actual video illustration of the principle, I understood it better. And I wrote the script! So that's just proof of how powerful it is to make complex concepts visual and simple.

Whiteboard videos also have a playful, disarming quality to them, which helps lower people's defenses. Sometimes financial information can be threatening or intimidating. But when packaged in this kind of entertaining, simple format, it's easier to learn and understand complex information. These videos have the added benefit of making dry topics more interesting, because the constant movement of the drawing hand and the images taking shape keeps viewers engaged.

3. Educate, Don't Sell = Content Marketing

The kinds of videos Kevin and Alicia are using aren't "selling" anyone. The videos are educating them. This is the new direction of marketing. It's called Content Marketing, and it means that you provide valuable content to attract your ideal clients to you. When you answer the questions they're asking themselves, you'll be a valuable resource for them.

4. Shareable & Search Engine Friendly

This kind of content also has the benefit of being shareable (through email and social media) and search engine friendly (through blogging and YouTube searches), because these are the questions people are typing into google searches.

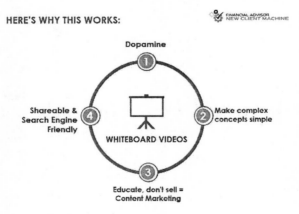

Figure 4.1 Whiteboard animated videos engage prospective clients for financial advisors in a unique way. They stimulate the release of dopamine, the "happiness" chemical, in the prospective client's brain through the drawing process. They also make complex concepts simple through entertaining, educational content marketing.

This type of Content Marketing is the direction everything is going now. The old style of selling is dead. The new way to attract clients is to provide entertaining, educational content to magnetically draw them to you. And the awesome thing is, I know this is what you love to do already. You're an educator at heart, and this type of marketing strategy enables you to start demonstrating your knowledge and expertise to your new clients online before you ever even meet them.

Younger Advisors coming up understand this intuitively. Millennials grew up with this stuff. It's like their mother tongue to understand the internet and how to make connections online.

They're practically born with a mobile device in hand, and the internet is their native tongue.

So that's what they're going to use in their business practices to beat you out. That's your competition, and it's only going to get more intense as a flood of young new advisors enter your space every year and start taking market share from more experienced advisors who just can't find a way to connect with their clients on the internet.

Millennials are now the largest generation in the workforce, and as they continue to accumulate wealth throughout their careers, these will be the people you're targeting as your prospective clients as well. So you need to be interacting with them the way THEY want to interact. And how they want to interact is through the internet.

So this is what you're going to learn in this book: how you can get up to speed quickly and easily with new Content Marketing strategies so you don't get left behind and beat out by younger advisors before you even know what hit you.

As you keep up with the times and adapt to a changing landscape in your practice, you're going to find that it's a lot easier and actually more fun that you might think. And you're going to position yourself to not be one of those advisors who finally just have to throw in the towel because you just never figured out how to get that steady stream of clients coming in your door. Instead, you'll find that people are calling you, instead of you having to call them. And when you talk with potential new clients, they've already seen your content online, so you've got that credibility, authority, and even local star power that gives you higher status to close business more quickly and easily.

It really is magical how this kind of marketing strategy creates automatic respect for you and for your ability to help your clients with their most important financial problems.

So let's dive in to three simple keys that we'll unpack to help you finally get that steady stream of new clients coming in your door. When that starts to happen, it's like this buoyant effect where everything in life gets more enjoyable. You're having more fun working because you're not worried about where your next client is coming from, and that makes it easier to also enjoy your time off with no stress. You can really relish the fruits of your labors by taking that vacation you've been wanting to take for years. Or buying something really nice for someone you love. Or just having the satisfaction that your retirement is secure, as you help other people make their retirement secure.

So let's dive in now.

Chapter 5

3 Simple Keys to Grow Your Practice

The best and most cost-effective way to build your practice is to do 3 things:

Key #1: Keep the Clients You Have

Key #2: Get Referrals to New Clients

Key #3: Multiply Your Results through the Internet

We're going to start getting into the nitty gritty now, so you might want to pick up a highlighter or pen and start marking up this book with an eye toward how you'll get these strategies in place for your practice.

Key #1: Keep the Clients You Have

One great way to keep the clients you have is by providing them with educational and entertaining video content.

1. When you provide your current clients with this kind of content, this is a powerful **Value Add** for them, because you're adding to their financial education.

2. When you stay in touch with consistent, helpful content, it **shows you care**, you're making an effort.

3. It also builds **good will**, because your clients feel taken care of. You're providing an easy way to learn, and making them feel smarter.

4. This kind of automated video marketing strategy is much **more time-efficient** for you than individual calls or emails to them, and more enjoyable for them because they can consume the content at the most convenient time and at their own pace.

5. These video marketing strategies are also **resource-efficient** because you can use the same video across multiple platforms like email, social media, and blogging.

What this means for you is that when your current clients or prospects receive video content from you, they're more likely to engage with your content. When they engage with your content, they feel like they received value from you, they remember you, and they feel grateful to you. All these things will help cement your relationship with your current clients so you'll keep them for a very long time.

Key #2: Get Referrals to New Clients

Let's take just one of the marketing platforms I've been mentioning and drill down: your email newsletter to current clients.

1. According to Constant Contact, one of the leading email newsletter service providers in the US, videos are the **#1 thing you can do to increase your click through rate** in your emails.

   What this means for you is that your video content makes it much more likely that those receiving your emails will actually engage with your content. If they don't engage with your content, then your communication is not working. That's why it's so important to ensure that you have enjoyable, engaging content to share, so that your communication will actually be effective and not a waste of everyone's time.

   When you consistently provide entertaining, educational video content that your audience enjoys consuming, that keeps you top of mind with current clients, so they're more likely to refer you.

Although it would be nice to believe that our clients are always thinking about us and looking for ways to help us expand our businesses, it's just not true. People need to be reminded about you in order to remember you, and seeing your videos in an email or a social media post is a perfect way to stay top of mind so your clients can refer you.

2. When you've done something nice for someone over and over (like providing them with free educational videos they enjoy interacting with), they want to do something nice for you. This is called the **Law of Reciprocity**, and when used correctly, it's a powerful marketing tool. Your clients will feel compelled by a time honored network of obligation we all understand to return the favor. One form this might take is referring you to a friend, so this means that your Content Marketing can stimulate more referrals as a result of the Law of Reciprocity.

3. **Shareable**: When you provide entertaining, enjoyable content, your clients and prospects are much more likely to share it. They need to feel proud of the information they're sharing, because they're actually endorsing it by sharing it, and videos have that "coolness" factor that makes people love to share them. Email makes it so easy and quick to forward your videos.

4. **Call to Action:** One of the simplest principles of marketing that is often overlooked is that people will do what you ask them to do. We can't assume that people even know we want referrals. So we need to ask for them. The old adage is still in effect: "Ask and you shall receive."

So when you send out your valuable video content, *ask* your recipient to forward the email to one person they know who could benefit from this information. You'll be surprised how effective this simple technique can be.

I used this strategy to increase attendance on a recent webinar I hosted. I sent out an email to my whole email list and asked each person to forward the email to one financial advisor they knew who could benefit from the information I was planning to share. Within a couple hours I had 30 people email me back and say "Done!" They passed it on to a financial advisor they knew because I asked them to. People will do what you ask them to do, because people are gratified by being helpful. So make it easy for them to feel good about themselves. Ask for one specific action you'd like them to take.

BONUS: When you ask them to pass your content along, ask them to pass it along to a certain kind of person who fits your profile for your Ideal Client. For instance, if your Ideal Client is a professional woman between the ages of 40 and 60, you might do your Call To Action as below.

Here's an example of what you could write in the PS at the bottom of your email:

"Please take a moment to forward this email to one mature professional woman you know who could benefit from the information I've provided in this video. Thanks!"

So far, we've talked about how to keep the clients you already have and how to stimulate more referrals from your current clients.

In the two strategies we've already talked about, notice you're killing two birds with one stone. Your emails including videos to your clients will not only solidify those relationships and keep your clients close and loyal to you, they will also motivate them to give you referrals, because you're providing sticky, shareable content and asking them to share it.

Now let's talk about the game-changing element of the internet: the ability to effortlessly multiply your results.

Key #3: Multiply Your Results through the Internet

1. One of the greatest things about investing in **your own video content is that it's <u>leverageable</u>**. For each piece of video content you invest in creating, you can get multiple bounces out of it.

   You can use your video in your **blog posts** on your website. (We'll talk more about the tremendous Search Engine benefits of doing this later.)

   You can also share that same video on YouTube, Facebook, LinkedIn, Google+ and Twitter, just to name a few **social media platforms**.

   And we already talked about how to use your video in your **email newsletters**.

   Additionally, you can include links to your videos in your **email signature** and your **LinkedIn profile**, and you can promote your videos on **YouTube**.

   So we've just covered six different places on the internet you can use the same video. And when you have multiple videos, then **your online presence starts to multiply** as you continue to get at least six uses out of each video. So for instance, when our clients for our Turnkey Video System or Custom Video System (find more information about these products here: www.FinancialAdvisorNewClientMachine.com) get 24 one-minute videos, and each one of those videos gets six uses on six different platforms, we're already up to 144 places online that these videos will be found on the internet.

And that's not even including more sophisticated email autoresponder strategies, which we'll cover later in this book as well.

2. We talked above about how easy it is to share a video when you get it in the form of an email. But it's **even easier to <u>share</u> a video on social media.** With just one mouse click, your audience can share your videos with their whole audience. And this is where multiplication really starts to kick in.

The average person knows 200 people. So if you are connected to 200 people on Facebook, and each of those 200 people is connected to 200 people, you have a potential audience of 40,000 people with each social media post on Facebook. For free! So if even 1% of your audience shares your content, you're reaching 400 people. Again, this is totally free.

- The average person knows 200 people.

- Your 200 connections times each person in your audience's 200 connections = 40,000 person potential audience for your video content.

- If you have even just a 1% Share Rate, that's 400 people who saw your video content. For free.

And that's just within one social media platform, not all six platforms we talked about above.

Isn't it worth just a little effort to get in front of that many people?

3. These **shares are the equivalent of a <u>testimonial</u>**, which you as a financial advisor are not permitted to use. But when people share your video content online, it implies that they endorse you. It's the equivalent of a word of mouth referral, since it's being passed from friend to friend. So internet marketing strategies like these enable you to get testimonial-like endorsements in a way that your compliance department will approve.

So now we've talked about:

- How to keep the clients you have with a video strategy

- How to generate more referrals with a video strategy

- How to multiply your results on the internet with a video strategy

Chapter 6

Video: The Great Accelerator

N ow let's go a little deeper into how to multiply your results on the internet.

VIDEO: THE GREAT ACCELERATOR

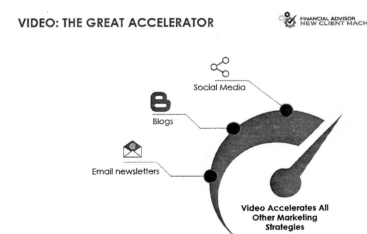

Figure 6.1 Video accelerates every other marketing strategy by making it more effective. When video is included in email newsletters, blogs, and social media, it exponentially increases the response rate on these marketing platforms.

Video accelerates every other marketing strategy.

You'll notice in everything we've talked about already that video is piggybacked on other marketing strategies, like email newsletters, blogging, and social media.

That's because video is the great accelerator. It makes every other marketing strategy you're using more effective.

So now we're going to talk about how to use video to accelerate each of these three marketing strategies:

1. Email newsletters

2. Blogs

3. Social media

But first, I'm going to tell you a story. This is my own true story of how my website started appearing on Google Page 1 from using video marketing strategies.

Case Study: How I Got on Google Page 1 with Video Blogging

When I started my business in 2009, I couldn't get on Google Page 1 to save my life. I remember clicking through google search results for search terms I was hoping my website would rank for, and even after page 20 of the search results, I hadn't found my website. It was not ranking in Google search engines at all. It just seemed so impossible to get found on Google.

About that time, I started offering a video package to my clients where I would film 24 1-minute videos of them all in one 3-hour shoot, so they could get a large volume of video content for an affordable rate. This Video SEO (Search Engine Optimization) Package is still available today. You can see the details at www.JillAddison.com/video-seo)

I had talked with a video producer on the East Coast who was offering this package and advising his clients to drip these videos out on their websites' blogs over time. So I decided to offer the same package to my clients on the West Coast. My first step was to test this strategy on my own website.

So I took all the video content I'd already produced and uploaded to YouTube for my business and started posting one video to my website's blog about every three days. Rather than come back and do this manually every three days, I used the handy scheduling feature in Wordpress (the platform my website is hosted on) and scheduled them all at once so they would drip out on autopilot. (You can watch a video tutorial about how to do this here: www.bit.do/SchedulingBlog)

A few weeks later, I got a Tweet (on Twitter) from a colleague who worked at a Search Engine Optimization (SEO) company. He said, "Did you know your website is climbing really fast in search engine results?"

By the third month, my website was ranking on Google Page 1 for 3 of my most competitive keywords.

Now that people could find me online when they needed the services I provide, **I started to get inbound phone calls from people who found me on Google.**

These inquiries from potential new clients had several advantages:

1. They were already actively searching online for my services, which means that they were very warm leads who were likely **ready to buy**.

2. Before they called me, they had most likely **already looked around my website and gotten familiar with me** through watching my videos and reading my content, and so they were that much farther down the road toward becoming my clients.

3. This is the best part: I didn't have to call them, **they called me**! It is so much nicer to be chased, than to chase, don't you think?

To see exactly how to use this strategy for your practice, watch the video tutorial here about how to automatically schedule You-

Tube videos to your website's blog over time: www.bit.do/YouTubeBlogStrategy)

This video will show you all the details of exactly how to use this video marketing strategy to get your own website found on Google.

CASE STUDY:

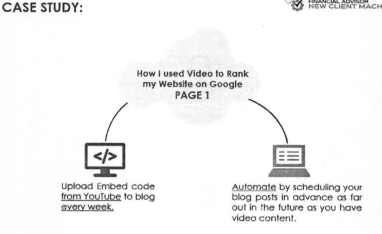

Figure 6.2 In this Case Study, you'll learn from the true story of how I transformed my website with video content from being lost and invisible on the internet to being found on Google Page 1, which generates inbound calls from warm prospects on a regular basis.

I have continued to upload one new video to my blog every week for several years now, and I continue to get inbound calls from warm leads on a regular basis from this strategy.

This is the only strategy I used to help my website be found on Google Page 1.

So instead of paying an expensive SEO company to help my website rank on Google with multiple strategies, I just continue to drip out videos on my blog, and that keeps me on Google Page 1 for my key search terms.

Blogging with your videos is one of the most valuable video marketing strategies for you, because it helps your website be found by the people who are searching for your services online. When your prospective clients find your website and engage with your videos and other written content before calling you, it creates authority and credibility for you, which is an essential key to actually converting these leads into clients.

Google search is not the only way this strategy will benefit you. When people are referred to you, often they will check you out on the internet before taking the next step toward meeting with you. So your online presence is an important link in the chain toward them becoming your client.

When they encounter you on your website, they must be "wowed." Your video library on your blog shows that you are serious about providing helpful financial education, which is what your prospective clients are looking for from you. It also shows that you are serious about your practice and you care enough to really invest in it by creating this kind of engaging, educational content for them.

All these things work together to help connect you with your prospective clients on the internet in a way that "wows" them and compels them to contact you to take the next step toward becoming your client.

And this is the whole purpose of marketing: to help each of your prospective clients move down the path toward becoming your client, one step at a time.

> **Warning: This strategy only works with YouTube Embed Codes.**

I have a colleague who tried this strategy but hosted his videos on a different video sharing site (Vimeo) and he did not see any measurable results.

You must use YouTube embed codes to see this strategy work. This is because Google owns YouTube, so naturally they are going to prioritize ranking YouTube content over other video sharing sites.

So that's a quick overview of how using YouTube videos in your website's blog will help your website be found in Google.

Now let's talk about email marketing and video.

Email Marketing and Video

Email marketing is one of the oldest forms of internet marketing. It's worked extremely well over the years, and it continues to be one of the most effective ways to use the internet to keep in touch with current clients and connect with new ones.

One of your most important assets in your business is your email list.

The easiest way to start building an email list is to compile the emails of all your clients and begin regular communication with them through email newsletters.

After you've got that in place, then you can start building your email list in a number of ways.

Ways to Build Your Email List

1. One easy way to build your email list is to **always get a business card from each new business contact you meet**, then email them to let them know you'd like to provide them with valuable financial educational information through your email newsletter, and add them to your list. (Or better yet, delegate this to your assistant.)

2. Another great way to build your list passively is to make sure you have an **Opt In form on your website's home page.** You can see an example of my Opt In form here: www.JillAddison.com. On the right of the page, you'll see where it says "Get Jill's 1-Minute Video Marketing Tip of the Month" and then a place to enter First Name and Email. You'll always want to collect these 2 essential pieces of information, since that will allow you to personalize your emails with their first name. But don't ask for more information than this, because every extra bit of information you request will reduce your Opt In rate. So only ask for the essentials: First Name and Email. We'll talk more about how to make the most of this Opt In strategy with video later in this book.

3. A third passive way to build your email list is to put an invitation to receive your content **below your signature in each outgoing email**. This means you will be promoting your email newsletter passively through the hundreds of emails you're already sending each month. We'll cover what to say in this invitation later in this book.

Here are several affordable <u>email newsletter services</u> you can consider to use this email newsletter strategy:

- **Constant Contact**—this is one of the oldest email newsletter services, and I think they've gotten a little too comfortable. They charge more and offer less.

- **MailChimp**—Mailchimp is perfect for a beginner because it offers fairly robust email newsletter services and is free if you have 2,000 contacts or less.

- **AWeber**—this software is more robust than MailChimp and Constant Contact. So if you are planning to really scale your email newsletters in the future, you may want to take a closer look at AWeber before you decide which service to start with.

According to Constant Contact, using the word "video" in the Subject line of your emails is the #1 way to increase your Open Rate. (An Open Rate is the percentage of recipients who open your email. Your Open Rate is a good measure of how engaged your audience is with your content.)

And according to Marketo (a major marketing automation software program), email that uses the word "video" for a direct Call to Action had a 53% higher click to open rate over email that did not mention video. In plain English, this means that when you use the word "video" in your email subject line, 53% more people will open it because people want to watch video. So if you're going to go to the trouble to include video in your email, for goodness sake, be sure to mention it in your email's Subject line. You'll get way more people opening your emails this way.

And after they open your emails and click on your videos, they'll have an enjoyable experience, because you're providing them with valuable information in an entertaining and engaging way.

When you do that, people are much more likely to actually forward your emails to others (i.e. refer you), because you're providing them with content they enjoyed, and they'll be sure someone else could enjoy that content and benefit from it too.

The psychology of why people share content with others has to do with association. People want to be associated with cool new trends, and video content for financial education fits that bill.

This sharing of cool content becomes especially important when it comes to social media. So now let's talk about social media and video.

Social Media and Video

Social media platforms include websites like Facebook, LinkedIn, Twitter, Google+, YouTube, Instagram, Pinterest, etc. Like most new trends, these sites started out popular with young people and have worked their way up to retirees. Now many teenagers have moved on to newer social media platforms like Snapchat and Vine. And many middle-aged and even retirement aged people are on social media like Facebook in order to see photos and keep updated on the lives of their younger family members. So these days, Facebook is often a great place to interact with your ideal client, even when they're older.

The beauty of social media platforms like Facebook is that they make it very easy to get started. They are extremely user friendly. They'll even suggest "people you might know" that you can connect with. They make these suggestions based on mutual acquaintances and friends. For instance, if you're connected to Bill and John, and Pete is also connected to Bill and John, Facebook will assume you might also know Pete and suggest that you connect with Pete as well. They can also search your contacts in your email (with your permission) to help you connect on the internet with people you're already friends with in real life.

This is an extremely powerful technique, as we saw earlier with Kevin's story of connecting on Facebook with an old friend from high school whose business was worth $200,000.00 +.

And if it's easy for people to forward your video content when it arrives in an email, it's ten times easier to share content on social media. It is literally a one click transaction that takes less than 4 seconds. They don't even have to think about who to share it with, because when they share something on social media, it's shared with everyone in that person's network. Amazing!

So again, like we talked about before, you have the potential of an average audience of 400 people with every social media post you share (see the math we did earlier in this book). And this is all free.

One reason why video is some of the best content you can post on social media is because many social media platforms will automatically post a thumbnail image when you post a YouTube video.

Here's an example of what a thumbnail image looks like:

Figure 6.3 When you post a video on the internet, many social media sites will automatically generate a thumbnail image, which catches people's eye and makes them want to click on your content.

A thumbnail image is just a still picture of your video, with a play button in the middle.

An image will naturally attract people's eye when they're looking through a social media newsfeed. And when it has the play button signaling video content, it becomes even more appealing, because people want to watch video.

So when you use video links in your social media posts, the thumbnail image that's automatically generated catches people's eye and makes them click to watch. And we all know that these days, people want to watch video more than they want to read.

Facebook and other social media sites know this, so they are focusing on video content. One way they're doing this on Facebook is that Facebook now automatically starts playing your video before people even click on it, which causes more people to click on it and watch it than if it was just a static image. You'll notice this as you scroll through your Facebook newsfeed, that the videos are already playing when you see them. When you click to play the video, then you can hear the audio as well.

Now let's talk about YouTube, the biggest (by far) video sharing website in the world.

Here are some statistics that will surprise you.

Chapter 7

A Closer Look at YouTube

YouTube has more than 1 Billion users. That's 1 in 7 people on earth. I bet you didn't know YouTube is that big, and it's only getting bigger.

For instance, a couple years ago, YouTube had 50% of the market share for video-sharing sites. Now it's almost 75%. And the number of hours people are watching YouTube videos each month is up 50% year over year. (source: YouTube.com) YouTube is growing at a phenomenal rate.

That's because people love to watch video on the internet; YouTube has a free service that people cannot get enough of. Another reason YouTube is so big is because Google owns YouTube.

YouTube is the #1 or #2 search engine in the world. I've actually been hearing people say that YouTube is the #1 search engine in the world, but frankly, I'm not sure how they're measuring that. It's hard to believe Google isn't still the #1 search engine in the world. But it's probably because they're measuring it by engagement. I wouldn't be at all surprised if people are spending more time engaging with content on YouTube than on Google, so by that measure, YouTube is #1. That makes sense, because video tends to engage people longer than any other type of medium. Once you start watching a video, you often keep watching it because it's interesting and engaging and you become absorbed in the content. So the engagement rate for video is much higher than any other medium like written text or photos.

But even if Google is still the #1 search engine in the world, YouTube is the #2 search engine. And you can't be on the #2 search engine in the world without video content. So this is yet another reason that you cannot afford to ignore video anymore.

Because Google owns YouTube, it prioritizes YouTube content in its search engine results over any other video sharing website. So not only can you rank in YouTube searches with video content, you can also rank in Google searches with video content from YouTube.

Here's the last piece of the puzzle of YouTube that I want to put together for you. And this is a very important piece of your video marketing strategy, so really pay attention to this. It is extremely important that you own your own video content, you don't just rent it from a subscription service. When you own your own videos, you can put them on YouTube, which enables you to be found on the 2nd biggest search engine in the world by your ideal client.

If you just rent content from a subscription service, you'll never be found on YouTube and you'll miss a huge chunk of internet traffic that's available only through YouTube. You'll never really get traction with your video marketing because you can't build on something you don't own. Just like real estate. If you're just renting your content through a subscription service that lets you use their videos, when you stop paying for that subscription, all your access to any video you've been using goes away instantly. So you're hamstrung, you can't build a long-term video strategy that keeps paying you back over time if you're just renting your video content. Because the second you stop paying, all your access goes away.

So this is very important: don't rent your video content, own it. When you own your video content and put it on YouTube, it will have a snowball effect and you'll get more and more views. I have over 120,000 Views on my YouTube channel from this snowball effect. And I consistently rank on Google Page 1 through posting my YouTube videos on my website's blog on a regular basis.

As you continue to evolve in your marketing, you'll begin using your videos in more sophisticated strategies, like email autoresponders. We'll go into that advanced strategy a little later in this book, but for now, just know that it's important that you position yourself now to grow into more advanced marketing strategies in the future. You can do this by making sure you own all your video content now so you can repurpose it over and over, long after your investment in your videos is paid in full.

Chapter 8

Summary

So let's review. You now understand that shifting your marketing focus to the internet is not only a good idea, it's pretty much mandatory. We've talked about how there are tens of thousands of new financial advisors coming online each year and they're naturally technology savvy because they grew up on the internet. It's like their native tongue.

But your experience and maturity is one advantage you have over these younger advisors who are trying to take your business. Where they might spend their time creating their own video content, you know the value of staying focused on your core competency and working smarter by outsourcing your marketing activities. So that's one important advantage you have.

As a result of everything you've learned in this book, you know that financial advisors who are not making the transition that everyone in this industry must make now to marketing on the internet will most likely be out of business in the next 3-5 years. It hurts me to tell you that, but you need to know that. I was just talking to one of my clients, Jake, who's a financial advisor in the Great Lakes region and he said the same thing. He said, "Advisors who aren't moving their marketing online will be out of business. Sooner than they think, they'll be extinct." That's how serious it is. Because the old ways just aren't working like they used to. I know you know that.

Every financial advisor I talk to on the phone tells me about this frustrating experience you're having. You used to be able to do a few seminars a year and have a nice living. Now you're barely breaking even on doing multiple seminars and you're working a lot harder. It's really frustrating. I know because I've talked with so many of you personally and I can hear the frustration in your voice.

Here's something you need to hear: the definition of insanity, according to Albert Einstein, is doing the same thing over and over and expecting different results.

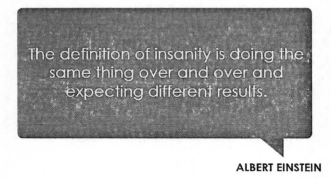

The definition of insanity is doing the same thing over and over and expecting different results.

ALBERT EINSTEIN

Why would you keep doing things you know aren't working well?

Why would you keep doing seminars without starting to make the transition to also marketing on the internet? You know that's where everything is going. It's obvious.

Maybe you're hoping that something will magically just change about your practice without you having to change anything. But that's not how life works. You are going to have to change if you want to survive and thrive in this business. And you can. You can do this.

So here are the benefits you can expect to receive from these video marketing strategies.

INTERNET MARKETING & ONLINE VIDEO:

Figure 8.1 Your video marketing strategies will help you close new business faster by elevating your status, credibility, authority and "local star power".

Video marketing will increase your status, give you credibility, authority and local star power that will attract your ideal clients to you and make it much easier to close new business. Your video strategies will also cause your current clients to refer business to you at a faster and faster rate.

From everything you've learned in this book, you can see that video is one of the most essential keys to help you stand apart from your competition.

Just sending out a market report email that no one reads and no one cares about, much less will forward to someone else, just isn't going to cut it anymore. You need highly entertaining and educational video content that will give you that critical edge over your competition.

So the question really isn't if you're going to use video in your marketing, it's how you're going to do it.

There are several ways to start generating your content for internet marketing. And some are better than others.

- You can create or film your videos yourself

- You can hire someone to shoot and edit videos you still do yourself by getting on camera

- Or you can invest in turnkey video solutions that allow you to keep doing what you do best, which is helping your clients reach their financial dreams and goals

Any of these approaches can work. And they can all add value to your marketing strategies.

One thing I will warn you about if you choose to create your videos yourself: video production is extremely time consuming. I do it for a living and I can't even believe how long it takes. It's an extremely time consuming process, and there's a long learning curve to get it right.

But if you have the interest and the time, you can try it. You can buy all the equipment and set up a video studio in your house or hire people to shoot you on video and edit your videos. When we're talking about having a video strategy that will work, that requires a lot of videos. And that's going to get very expensive, just so you know.

The easier and more cost-efficient way to get your video content handled is to choose a turnkey video solution, which will take a minimum of time and effort on your part and can often give you even better results than getting on camera yourself.

As a result of everything you've learned in this book, you know that if you do this, it can have a revolutionary impact on your practice. You won't get left behind as the world changes, and you'll adjust and thrive in this new internet world we live in.

In the next chapter, you'll learn about how turnkey video systems can make your life easier and help you attract your ideal client effortlessly on the internet.

Chapter 9

Turnkey Video Systems

Turnkey video systems can help you grow your practice in the following ways.

Turnkey video systems:

1. Help you generate a steady stream of new clients from the internet

2. Compel your current clients to refer new clients to you on a regular basis

3. Enable you to get these things with a minimum of time and effort from you

4. Position you to help more people with your expertise

5. Help you get certainty about where your next client is coming from

Whiteboard videos in particular are wildly popular because they're the most engaging type of video. People just love to watch them. There's actually a scientific reason for that. When we watch the images being drawn, at the moment of discovery when we see what the finished image will be, dopamine, the happiness chemical, gets released in our brains. We experience a burst of delight. And because people make buying decisions based on emotion, not logic, this lowers their defenses and puts your prospective clients in a happy state that's much more conducive to them taking the next step toward becoming your client.

Turnkey video systems make it **easy** for you to get these results. To see an example of how this is done, view a selection of whiteboard videos we've created as part of a Turnkey Video Library we created for financial advisors like you: www.bit.do/ FAPlaylist.

Most turnkey video systems feature static content, but some have flexibility. For instance, in our Turnkey Video System, we make any changes your compliance department requests. Like I mentioned earlier, we've cleared compliance departments with our videos at LPL Financial, Wells Fargo Advisors, and Guardian Life Insurance Company of America just to name a few, so compliance is not a problem.

Many turnkey video systems are subscription based, which means that the moment you stop paying for your content, your access to your videos stops. However, there are just a few turnkey video systems (actually I only know of one) that enable you to actually **own your video content**. Our Turnkey Video System includes upload of your videos, which you own, to your YouTube Channel every month and we even optimize them for search for you. YouTube is the 2nd biggest search engine in the world, so this is huge.

Later in this book, we'll walk you through step by step exactly how to get the biggest bang for buck from your turnkey videos through our **7 Steps to Video Marketing Success Process.** This process is responsible for the **amazing return on investment** that Alicia and Kevin and many others in the financial services industry are experiencing through online videos. With our 7 Steps to Video Marketing Success Process, we'll walk you through step by step how to promote your videos to your email newsletter list, your social media and on your blog, as well as some other easy tips that can fast forward your results.

Here's an overview of our 7 Steps to Video Marketing Success:

1. Upload your videos to **YouTube,** the 2nd biggest search engine in the world, and optimize for search

2. Post your videos to your website's **blog** to help your website rank higher in search engine results

3. Post your videos on **social media sites** like Facebook, LinkedIn, Twitter, and Google+

4. Include a link to your videos in your **email newsletter**

5. Include a link to your videos in your **email signature**

6. Post your videos on your **LinkedIn Profile**

7. Promote your videos on your **YouTube** Channel

In the last part of this book, we'll walk you through exactly how to implement each of these 7 Steps to Video Marketing Success, complete with screenshots and links to video tutorials, so look at those chapters as a "how to" manual. You can hand this book to your assistant and then they should have everything they need to keep these marketing strategies running smoothly for you month after month.

But let's get back to the first step now, which is to get your video content secured and uploaded to YouTube with a turnkey video system.

It's natural to feel a tension between wanting to secure an easy turnkey solution for your video marketing, but still wanting the video content to be customized to reflect your exact niche. This is a difficult tension to navigate, since most video systems are either turnkey and require very little involvement from you, or they're customized and involve a significant investment of your time.

The other tension to navigate is that often templated videos are affordable, while custom videos are expensive.

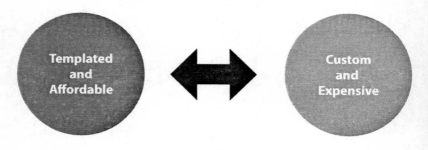

Figure 9.1 Financial Advisors often feel like they have to choose between a templated video solution that's affordable, or a custom video solution that's expensive.

Our Turnkey Video System provides the best of both worlds, in that you can make it as turnkey or as customized as you like.

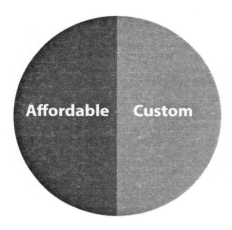

Figure 9.2 Only one turnkey video system provides the ease of an affordable turnkey solution combined with the personalization of a customized approach. Learn more here: www.FAVideoTraining.com

Both approaches have their strengths.

With a turnkey approach, you save time so you can focus on what you do best: helping your clients live out their financial dreams.

With a customized approach, you laser target your ideal client by creating content that appeals directly to them.

As with most things in life, a little variety is often the best solution. By combining a turnkey approach for some videos, with a customized approach for other videos, you'll get the best of both worlds.

Here's what's going to happen when you get these videos. These videos are going to help you grow your practice by communicating better with your prospects and existing clients and generating more referrals. They'll make you stand out from the crowd, and showcase how you're special and unique. That means you're able to help more people, you're able to provide better for your family, take trips, take time off, give to charity, send your kids to the college you want, or whatever more money and more success means to you. It also means that you'll feel confident about your business and its growth potential in this new millennium. You'll feel successful, and you'll enjoy the novelty of getting clients in an effortless new way.

When your confidence increases, that's going to impact every area of your business and personal life and take you to new levels of success and satisfaction. Because of this increased confidence from your new marketing, you'll attract even more new clients and your brain will be freed to create even better financial plans for them, which results in a virtuous cycle of ever increasing abundance and prosperity for you and for them.

It feels magical, like you're riding the wave, and your clients will feel that from you too. You'll rub off on them as you help dozens, and then hundreds and even thousands of clients stop worrying about retirement because they have a plan. And as that plan is lived out and financial abundance follows, that will provide joy and opportunity for everyone in their sphere of influence, like their children and charitable causes they support. And then think about all the people THOSE people will impact in a positive way. The numbers really start to add up, and pretty soon we're talking about your influence reaching to tens of thousands of people.

Free Bonus with This Book

This free bonus will position you to experience this kind of impact through your life and practice.

To claim your spot in your free 60-minute Online Video Training Seminar (Value: $295) with Jill Addison, visit:

www.FAVideoTraining.com

Continuing education credits may apply for you.

In this Online Video Training Seminar, I personally walk you through the best techniques and strategies to maximize the power of online video to grow your financial advisory practice.

You'll hear case studies you can't hear anywhere else, and glean valuable insights for how to replicate those successes in your own business.

You'll Learn:

- How to make people pre-disposed to become your client before you ever meet with them

- How to motivate your clients to refer you to new clients on a regular basis

- How to make your clients LOVE you even more and naturally refer you at a faster and faster rate

- 3 keys to keep your current clients happy

- How to create an online presence that moves people several steps along in your sales process before you ever even talk with them in person

- How to build authority, credibility and celebrity with your video content

- One sneaky little trick that will make it impossible for your clients NOT to refer you

- The one single thing that will make the difference between them referring you or not referring you

- A covert ops way to get testimonial-type credibility that your compliance department will not blink an eye at

- How to strategically get 5-7 bounces out of each video

- How video accelerates every other marketing strategy you have, so it's not just one tool, it's like a super tool that makes every other tool more effective

- How to take your current real life relationships onto the internet, and also how to take your internet relationships into real life relationships

- Why video is working so well, in case you're one of the few who are still skeptical about video

- Our story of how video helps us get calls from people we don't even know, who were referred by people we don't even know, all because of our videos

- And More

This Online Video Training Seminar is free for you as the owner of this book, but be sure to claim your spot right away, since we're not sure how long this training will be available at the link below.

Visit www.FAVideoTraining.com **today to get access to your FREE Bonus
60-Minute Online Video Training Seminar.**

Chapter 10

7 Steps to Video Marketing Success

The rest of this book is devoted to getting into the nitty gritty of how to apply the 7 Steps to Video Marketing Success Process to your practice to see maximum results from your internet and video marketing strategies. You'll find step-by-step instructions with screenshots and links to video tutorials that will answer all your questions.

This training section of the book also equips you to easily and efficiently delegate all these strategies to an assistant so you can stay focused on what you do best: helping your clients live their dreams through the exceptional financial planning services you provide.

Each of the next 7 chapters will provide all the answers you need about how to incorporate the 7 Steps to Video Marketing Success into your practice to get the results you want.

7 Steps to Video Marketing Success

1. Upload your videos to **YouTube,** the 2nd biggest search engine in the world, and optimize for search

2. Post your videos to your website's **blog** to help your website rank higher in search engine results

3. Post your videos on **social media sites** like Facebook, LinkedIn, Twitter, and Google+

4. Include a link to your videos in your **email newsletter**

5. Include a link to your videos in your **email signature**

6. Post your videos on your **LinkedIn Profile**

7. Promote your videos on your **YouTube** Channel

Chapter 11

Step 1

Upload Your Videos to YouTube

Uploading your videos to YouTube is very simple. (If you've already invested in our Turnkey Video System, then we're doing this step for you and you can skip this chapter.)

First, you'll need a YouTube Channel. (A "Channel" is another name for an "Account" on YouTube.) We will create a YouTube Channel for you if you are a member of our Turnkey Video System or Custom Video System. If you are not yet a member of our programs, you can create your own YouTube channel.

After you're logged into your YouTube Channel, you'll see an Upload button in the upper right that looks like this:

Figure 11.1 To upload videos to YouTube, just log in to your YouTube account, then click the Upload button in the upper right corner on your screen.

Click on the Upload button and then you'll see a big arrow that looks like this:

Select files to upload

Or drag and drop video files

Figure 11.2 After you click on the Upload button, you'll see an image that looks like this. Simply click on the video file you'd like to upload, hold down the mouse button and drag the video file over this image. Then release the mouse button and your video will begin to upload.

You'll need to have your video file in one of the formats listed below:

- .mov
- .mpeg4
- .mp4
- .avi
- .wmv

- .mpegps

- .flv

- .WebM

> **Advanced Pro Tip: Make sure to title your video with a keyword rich title before you upload it. Keywords are the words you want to be found for on YouTube and Google. So an example might be "Financial Planning (Your City Here)".**

When you title your video file with a keyword rich title before uploading it, you'll get 2 advantages:

1. Titling your raw data (your video file) provides just one more way YouTube and Google can access data about your video in order to place your video in their search engine results.

2. YouTube will automatically fill in the Title of your video on YouTube with the title of the video file you uploaded. This saves you the extra step of having to type in the title to YouTube.

To see a 1-minute video tutorial about how to upload your video to YouTube, visit this link:

www.bit.do/UploadYouTubeVideo

To see a 4-minute video tutorial about how to make sure your videos can be found by search engines (Search Engine Optimization, or SEO) visit this link: www.bit.do/YouTubeSEO

Here's an overview of the information you'll learn about how to optimize your video for search (Search Engine Optimization) in the video above.

How to Optimize your Video for Search Engines

As mentioned above, be sure to title your video with a keyword rich title BEFORE you upload it to YouTube. This will help search engines like Google and YouTube see more data about your video, which will help them rank you in their search results.

There are 3 main areas you'll need to fill out when you upload your video to make sure search engines can see information about it in order to rank it in their search engines results:

1. Title

2. Description box

3. Tags

How to Title your YouTube Video

Make sure your title is **keyword rich** for search engines. But don't just type a string of keywords, since this isn't appealing to humans. Choose a title that incorporates your keywords for search engines, but also appeals to humans when they see your video online. This will ensure that search engines can find and rank your content, and that when humans see your content they'll want to click on it to watch it. An example of a title that's **friendly to both search engines and humans** is: "Financial Advisor Atlanta-Get Your Financial Questions Answered Here"

Notice that I worked the word "Financial" into the title twice. This is a best practice, so repeat one keyword in your title.

Also, notice I mentioned a specific city. This will mean you're only competing with financial advisors in your city or region for search engine results, instead of every financial advisor in the world.

All these tactics will increase the chances that your ideal client will find you in search engines.

Description box

At the top of your Description box, type your website address. Be sure to put http:// in front of your website, because this makes it a clickable link. You want to make it as easy as possible for people to get from YouTube to your website, so list your website address first thing and make it clickable by putting http:// at the beginning, like this: http://www.FinancialAdvisorNewClientMachine.com

Below your website, type your phone number. This is part of making your YouTube video not only search engine friendly, but also human friendly. Some people would rather just pick up the phone and call you, so make it easy for them to do that by including your phone number.

Below these two pieces of contact information, fill in a description of your video. If you used a script to create your video, then the easiest way to do this is to simply copy and paste your script into the Description box.

Here's how to do this: go to your script in a Word document. If you're on a PC, press Ctrl A to Select All. Then press Ctrl C to Copy. Then go to the YouTube Description box and click to put your curser under your phone number. Then press Ctrl V to Paste. And voilà, your description box is fully optimized with a script that's keyword rich for search engines and friendly to human readers too. And it only took a few seconds, since you repurposed your script as your Description in YouTube.

Tags

The tags section is where you fill in your Keywords.

Remember, keywords are the words or phrases you're hoping to be found for online when people type these words or phrases into Google or YouTube search engines.

You don't need more than about 10 tags. The first tags will be weighted much more heavily than the later ones, so it's not necessary to have a ton of keywords. You just need to tag your video with 5-10 long tail keywords. A "long tail keyword" refers to a phrase instead of just one word. An example of a long tail keyword is "Financial Advisor Atlanta."

Be consistent. Use the same words in the Title, Description and Tags. This signals to search engines that this really is about this topic, since they keep seeing the same words everywhere on this video.

It's best to use phrases, what we call "long tail keywords", instead of just single words. For instance, if you tagged a video with "Finances, Planning, Atlanta", this does not give search engines quality information, since they'll be searching for each of those extremely broad terms independently of each other. However, if you tag your video with "Financial Planning Atlanta", now you have a long tail keyword that helps search engines understand what this video is about. It's not about just Finances, or just Planning, or just Atlanta, it's about Financial Planning in Atlanta.

The riches are in the niches, and when you target a niche, like a geographic area and a niche service like financial planning, now your chances of being found in search engines are much higher. If you get even more niche, like focusing just on long term care insurance, for instance, your chances of being found online go up even more.

Remember, you're competing with the whole world to get on Page 1 of searches in Google or YouTube. So you're not going to get there with really broad terms, because there's too much competition. But if you can niche down and optimize your videos for niche terms in certain geographic regions, then your competition is exponentially reduced and you have a chance of ranking on Page 1 of search engines.

When was the last time you went to Google Page 2? Page 1 is really all that usually matters, because people usually don't go on to Google Page 2, so you need to stack the odds in your favor that you could appear on Google Page 1, even if it's only to a very small audience of people searching on your long tail, niche keywords. You only need a few people to click on this to make it all worth it anyway, so don't be afraid to be super niche in your Tags.

To see these ideas in action, visit this link to watch a 4-minute video tutorial about how to make sure your videos can be found by search engines (Search Engine Optimization, or SEO): www.bit.do/YouTubeSEO

Chapter 12

Step 2

Post your videos to your website's blog to help
your website rank higher in search engine results

This is one of the most important ways to use your videos. Remember the story I told you earlier in this book about how I ranked my website on Google Page 1 for my most competitive keywords with this video blogging strategy? You can use videos to rank your website higher in search engines too.

If you don't already have a website, you must get one right now. Your website is the hub of all your marketing. You'll be driving all your internet traffic back to your website, so this is the heart of your marketing strategy. If you don't yet have a website, I highly recommend you get one through www.WebsiteIn5days. com. I personally know Chris Martinez, the owner, and he has a great system very similar to mine where his team can provide customized marketing solutions for a very low cost per month. Be sure to tell him I sent you.

With the Wordpress websites you can get at www.WebsiteIn-5days.com, a blog comes included in the website. If you're not sure what a blog is, it's a page on your website where you can post articles or videos and they're displayed on your website in a newsfeed type format. This is a way for you to continue to add fresh consistent content to your website.

The reason this blogging strategy with video works so well is because 1) Google has always loved fresh consistent content and 2) now Google also loves video. So when you put those two things together, you're going to get amazing Search Engine Optimization results.

What do we mean by consistent? We mean weekly blog posts. If you only post to your blog once a month, you'll get about 10% of the value of this strategy. If you post to your blog weekly, you'll get about 90% of the value. Consistency means weekly.

The nice thing about blogging is that you can incorporate all kinds of content.

You can provide some written content, and some video content. So if you've invested in our Turnkey Video System or our Custom Video System, you'll get 2 videos each month from us. You can post one to your blog right away, then schedule the other one to post in 2 weeks. That way you'll have a steady stream of video content twice a month, every month.

You can fill in the other 2 weeks each month with written content you write, or that you have someone else write for you. One very easy way to get this content is to re-use content you've already used in your email newsletter. Or you can repurpose other people's content by linking to it or embedding it on your blog. Repurposing your own or other people's content is a very efficient way to continue to provide valuable content to search engines and humans.

Don't make this harder than it has to be. Repurposing other people's content on your blog means you can even embed other people's videos to your blog. This is a smart technique because video blogging seems to get better results than written blogs.

A word of warning: do NOT just copy other people's content and paste it on your blog. That will get you slapped by Google, and it's not a nice thing to do. Instead, write a paragraph about why you think their content is valuable, then link to it or embed it on your blog. This is doing them a favor too because then they get an inbound link, which helps their search engine results. And it helps you too, because they just provided valuable content for you to share on your blog.

If you have a Wordpress website, it's very simple to schedule your blogs to post on a regular basis. I recommend that you always try to schedule your blogs in advance, so you don't run the risk of being inconsistent. When you schedule a large amount of content all at once, that's much more time-efficient. It also helps you stay consistent, which is essential for Search Engine Optimization results and for seeing results in your marketing from human beings who encounter you on the internet.

If you try to come back to this every week, chances are that life will get in the way, and then your strategy won't work because you weren't consistent. So use the tools available to you to be time-efficient and ensure consistency by scheduling your blog posts in advance. It is a pain in the butt to have to do this every week. So just delegate it to your assistant to schedule your blog posts monthly. Then you won't have to think about it or come back to it, it will just run on autopilot. Or if you really get organized, compile all your content for 6 months and just have your assistant schedule it all out twice a year.

Here's a comprehensive 4-minute video tutorial about how to schedule your blog posts on Wordpress so you can schedule them out in advance: www.bit.do/SchedulingBlog

Chapter 13

Step 3

Post your videos on social media sites like Facebook, LinkedIn, Twitter, and Google+

Much like blogging, it is really time consuming to come back and post to your social media sites every few days. But you don't have to do that. Instead, take advantage of the tools available to schedule your social media posts in advance.

Here's a system that has served me well for years.

My social media strategy is to post valuable content every 3 days or so to all my social media platforms, including several Facebook pages, my LinkedIn profile, my Google+ account and several Twitter profiles. But instead of coming back and doing this manually every 3 days (which would take forever!), I just compile all my posts every couple of months, and then I send them to my Virtual Assistant to schedule for me all at once.

I have her schedule these posts using **Hootsuite**. Hootsuite is a social media aggregator. That means that you can connect it to all your social media sites and it will allow you to post to all of them with one click. So instead of logging into all these social media sites separately (which again, takes forever), she just logs into one site, Hootsuite.

Hootsuite also enables you to schedule your social media posts in the future. This means that you don't have to come back to it all the time. You just sit down once every couple months and compile a big list of status updates, then send them to your Virtual Assistant and ask them to schedule your posts every 3 days out into the future.

Here's a quick video tutorial on how to schedule your You-Tube videos as status updates on all your social media sites using Hootsuite: www.bit.do/Hootsuite

When you post links to your videos on your social media sites, your Status Update could say something like this: "Check out my new 1-minute video: (link to your blog page with the video on it or straight to your video on YouTube)"

Here's an example of the kind of email I send to my Virtual Assistant every couple of months:

Hi Dianne,

Please schedule these as social media posts to all my social media sites (EXCEPT my personal Facebook profile*) using Hootsuite.

Schedule them to release one post every 3 days.

Schedule each post for 7am PST.

Please use the link shortener in Hootsuite for each link.

1. 4 Digital Marketing Trends for 2014: http://www.marketingprofs.com/opinions/2014/24242/four-digital-marketing-trends-to-watch-in-2014?adref=nlt012814

2. The Next Big Thing in Marketing: http://socialmediatoday.com/jamesgross/2255781/next-phase-marketing-technology-all-about-content?utm_source=smt_newsletter&utm_medium=email&utm_campaign=newsletter&inf_contact_key=18a4d57fc4549a1ca18d988a9499e-7cd797738e1b08b14b4f69b0906affc4f96

3. How to create effective Content Marketing. Awesome article: http://socialmediatoday.com/expresswriters/2079331/

content-marketing-vs-copywriting-top-strate-
gies-2014?utm_source=smt_newsletter&utm_me-
dium=email&utm_campaign=newsletter&inf_contact_
key=31c1a047ab0156aa512f0ee68405f0b53484035b-
546d44ec1c24addbdd80db9c

4. One of the best infographics I've seen. It's about Old vs
New SEO=What Works Now: http://socialmediatoday.
com/irfan-ahmad/2112491/sustainable-seo-meth-
ods-and-tools-work-2014?utm_source=smt_newslet-
ter&utm_medium=email&utm_campaign=newslet-
ter&inf_contact_key=9255a517a851f18f8e1816d-
67782f829c528eeccbd0ec839f46d3a37594677ab

5. How Companies are using Content Marketing
Now: http://socialmediatoday.com/pawan-desh-
pande/2102206/top-content-marketing-priori-
ties-and-challenges?utm_source=smt_newsletter&utm_
medium=email&utm_campaign=newsletter&inf_
contact_key=1054acdc7afa354b50c1952aeb97a-
f785aa831f692f3027c8d240c9f81db1714

6. Interesting article on the power of Purging your Office:
http://www.alibrown.com/blog/2014/03/20/to-attract-
the-new-and-better-purge-the-old-and-stagnant-by-ali-
brown/?inf_contact_key=0419a1c95ef3136212eced-
9c2646e74d0c7222a5dbf92f4a6b5e2e1a5806b491

7. (etc. etc.)

*I don't have my Virtual Assistant post to my Facebook personal profile this often because the expectations on Facebook personal profiles are that it will be 80% personal and only about 20% business. So I try to post pictures and information about my personal life on my Facebook personal profile most of the time, and just an occasional business post.

Notice that I'm not actually generating any new content for these social media posts. I'm just using links to articles I think my audience would find helpful. Again, this is the principle of repurposing content, and it will make your life so much easier.

I'm guessing you probably spend a fair amount of time educating yourself about your industry. In fact, you probably already have a file of articles you've found helpful or interesting. So you could mine all that content and use it for your social media posts.

If you don't currently have the links to the articles you've been saving from your internet research, then start saving links to articles as you find them going forward. Or instead of sharing links, you can also just pull out relevant facts or statistics that can be shared in one sentence and use those for your social media posts.

The goal is to provide valuable content (wherever it originates) and stay top of mind. You don't have to create all this content yourself. You can just repurpose other people's content and share that online. Even if no one clicks on your links, they're still seeing your face and your name in their social media feed, and that is keeping you top of mind. When you're top of mind, it's easier for others to refer you. This is the whole point of doing this: to stay top of mind and be perceived as someone with valuable information to share. So again, be consistent with this strategy, and it will serve you well. It will keep you top of mind with clients and prospects, which will help them take the next step to refer you or move toward becoming your client.

Remember, marketing is a journey. It's a lot like dating. It doesn't happen all at once, it happens gradually over time. You don't go on one date and say "Let's get married!" It's a gradual, step by step process of getting to know each other, liking each other more, and then finally making a commitment. It's the same with your marketing. So remember, your goal with all your marketing, including these social media posts, is just to help the people in your circles of influence take the next small step toward becoming your client, or referring others to become your client. It might not produce immediate results, but as you're consistent over time, it will produce results for you.

Here's one way social media has worked for me.

Over the years, I've built my social media network in several ways:

1. I accept everyone who wants to connect with me on LinkedIn, and I reach out to connect with new people who I think could be good partners for me.

2. I connect with people I've met personally on LinkedIn. Every time I meet a new person, I get their business card. Then when I get back to my office, I send them a request to connect on LinkedIn. This helps take my real relationships onto the internet where I can keep in touch and stay top of mind pretty effortlessly though consistently posting to LinkedIn where I know my network is watching my posts.

3. As I post consistently to social media platforms, new people find me and request to connect to me.

After years of doing this, I have an online network of 5,000+ people, so when I post, lots of people see it. It takes some time to build this up, but it's worth it.

Here's one example of results I've seen from social media: I've been promoting my webinars through my social media channels and I'm getting a 30% Opt In rate for my webinars through social media. That's 4 times more than an average opt in rate (7%).

I think the reason social media works so well is that it really is relational. As people see your posts over time, they feel like they know you (especially if you're sharing videos featuring your face and voice). When people feel like they know you, like you and trust you, they'll respond to you, even on the internet.

I know some people feel like they know me even though we only know each other on the internet. But there are other people who have been real relationships in my life that I keep in touch with by posting consistently to my social media channels.

Remember the story you heard earlier in this book about how one financial advisor, Kevin, got a client worth $200,000.00+ because of one Facebook post? She was a friend from high school that he was connected to on Facebook, and she just didn't realize how he could help her as a financial advisor until she saw one of his videos on Facebook. See her comment here:

Figure 13.1 Leveraging your real, existing relationships by connecting with them on the internet and then posting sticky, engaging content can lead to new business worth hundreds of thousands of dollars for you, like it did for Kevin from this one Facebook post.

After this conversation started on Facebook, it became a real conversation on the phone and in person, and then she became a real client worth over $200,000.00.

That's the power of maximizing relationships you already have and making new relationships on the internet.

> **To learn how to put your social media posting on autopilot, watch this quick video tutorial on how to schedule your YouTube videos as status updates on all your social media sites with one click using Hootsuite:** www.bit.do/Hootsuite

This video makes it very easy for you to delegate this to your assistant. Just send them instructions and status updates like the ones I sent to my virtual assistant and a link to this video tutorial. Then they should be all set to schedule your social media posts every 3 days out into the future to keep you top of mind with your social media networks.

Chapter 14

Step 4

Include a link to your videos in your email newsletter

If you're going to go to the trouble to put a video in your email newsletter, be sure to use the word "video" in your Subject line, since this will increase your Open Rate. People want to watch video more than they want to read, so make sure people are alerted to the valuable video content in your email so they'll open it.

Here's an example of how this works. One time I saw someone at a networking event who said to me, "I got your email and it said '1-Minute Video' in the Subject line and that's the only reason I opened it. I'm really busy, but I do have one minute, and I love videos."

After people open your email, increase the chances that they'll click on your video by including a thumbnail image. A thumbnail image is just a still picture of your video with a Play button on top of it.

Here's an example of a thumbnail image:

Figure 14.1 When you include video content in your email newsletters, be sure to include a thumbnail image like this one. A thumbnail image is a still picture from your video with a play button over it. These images catch the reader's eye and make them want to click to view your videos.

If you are using MailChimp, Constant Contact, or a similar email newsletter system, you can upload your image to your email and then link it to your video. Watch the video tutorial here to see how to do it: www.bit.do/EmailVideoThumbnail

Here are the steps:

1. Upload your thumbnail image as an image in your email message.

Then hyperlink that image to your video, so when they click on the image, the viewer will be taken to your video (which could be on your website or on YouTube, whichever you choose).

2. Also include a hyperlink in the text (example: "Click here to watch my new 1-minute video.") The more links you have to your video, the most likely people are to watch it.

3. Watch this quick video tutorial about how to upload images to your email newsletter and then link them to your video on YouTube here:

www.bit.do/EmailVideoThumbnail

By following this process, you'll create a seamless experience for your viewers. They'll just click on your thumbnail image in your email newsletter and then the video will pop up and play in YouTube.

Chapter 15

Step 5

Include a link to your videos in your email signature

Here's one of the easiest ways to get a lot of mileage out of your video content. Simply include a link to one of your videos in your email signature.

I've gotten over 2,500 Views on one of my videos using this strategy. It took a couple years of having this same email signature in my emails, but over time, the Views on YouTube can really add up.

Here's an example of how that signature looked:

> Jill Addison
> Online Video Producer
> President
> Jill Addison, Inc.
> mobile: (619) 850-5835
> www.JillAddison.com
> www.FinancialAdvisorNewClientMachine.com
>
> To watch an example of Turnkey or Custom Whiteboard Videos that can help you grow your Financial Advisory practice, click here:
> https://www.youtube.com/watch?v=72S4-XVhjpg

And the best part about this strategy is, it's totally passive. With every email you send out, you are sending out links to your videos that people can click on to find out more about you.

When they click on your links and watch your YouTube videos, you start to rack up more and more Views on YouTube. As you get more Views, YouTube sees that you have valuable content people want to watch, and it starts sending more traffic to your videos. You'll start to rank higher in Related Videos that appear to the right of video content in YouTube. And it will start to snowball.

I have over 120,000 Views on my videos on my YouTube channel, and I can assure you, I did not work for all those Views. I just put some strategies like this in place and kept uploading consistent videos, and then YouTube started to reward me with more and more traffic to my YouTube channel.

Getting more Views on YouTube is just one strategy to promote your videos, you need to employ all the strategies we're talking about in this book to get the most bang for buck.

It's just like everything else in life: every little decision matters. Every little marketing effort matters. It all starts to add up, just like when people save $200 every month. It doesn't seem like a lot each month, but when you're consistent over time, it really adds up and makes a difference. The same thing is true with your marketing. Just put these strategies in place and be consistent with all these little efforts over time, and it will start to really pay you back with interest…with how interested people are in your services. Sorry, I couldn't resist that pun. And I don't even like puns.

Advanced Pro Tip: If you want to really maximum this email signature strategy, then **use a link from a Playlist on YouTube.** When you use a Playlist link, then YouTube will automatically queue up your next video each time one of your videos ends. I have literally watch 30 minutes of content on YouTube I wasn't even that interested in just because someone was smart enough to use Playlists. It's like I got hypnotized into continuing to watch this endless stream of video. You can use this strategy to your advantage too, to keep more people engaged in your content and rack up more and more Views on YouTube.

Here's a video tutorial about how to use YouTube Playlist links: www.bit.do/YouTubePlaylists

Chapter 16

Step 6

Post your videos on your LinkedIn Profile

You will stand out from the crowd when your LinkedIn profile has a video embedded in it. How many financial advisors do you know who have a video on their LinkedIn profile? Don't miss this opportunity to stand out from the crowd and make a positive first impression.

It's super simple. Here's how to add a video to your LinkedIn profile.

1. Go to your LinkedIn profile

2. Hover over Profile in the navigation bar

3. From the dropdown, click Edit Profile

4. Then hover over the upper right corner of the Summary box. You'll see a little box appear with a + sign. Click on that box.

5. Then paste the link to your YouTube video in the field that appears. Then click the Continue button.

And voila, your LinkedIn Profile is instantly more personal and professional than 90% of your competition.

Watch this video tutorial about exactly how to embed a YouTube video in your LinkedIn profile:

www.bit.do/LinkedInProfileVideo

Chapter 17

Step 7

Promote your videos on your YouTube Channel

Now that you have YouTube videos, you can be found more ways online: on YouTube AND on Google, since Google can index your YouTube videos in its searches as well.

The next step to multiply your results is to promote your videos on YouTube.

Here are some quick and easy strategies to promote your videos on YouTube.

I suggest sending an email with a link to one of your YouTube videos to friends, family, colleagues, customers, newsletter lists, etc., and asking them to consider taking the following actions:

- Comment on the video

- Favorite the video

- Share the video

- Embed the video on their own website's blog (include an Embed code for them)

- Post a link to your video as one of their status updates on their social media

I recommend giving them text so it makes it very easy for them to take action. For instance: "Check out my friend's new 1-minute video. Very cool! (link to your video here)" (You can shorten this link for social media status updates by using a link shortener website like bit.do.)

You might want to send this email to a short list of people you're closest to, since they're the most likely to help you out.

Chapter 18

Bonus Strategies

Now we've covered all 7 Steps to Video Marketing Success and so you are fully equipped to maximize the value of your YouTube videos to get new clients.

Here are some additional bonus strategies to further maximize your video marketing strategies.

Bonus Strategy #1: Get an Assistant to Leverage Your Marketing

Remember, you don't have to do this all by yourself. In fact, you probably shouldn't. If you don't already have one, I highly recommend you hire an assistant (this could be a Virtual Assistant you hire on the internet) to help you implement all these strategies. I've hired several of my assistants and key sub-contractors through a website called Upwork, so check that out:

www.Upwork.com.

Now that you have this book in your hands, it's easy to just give this book to your assistant and have him or her implement all these strategies for you.

Don't make this harder than it has to be. You've already done the hardest part, which is just getting your videos on YouTube. Now all that's left is to make the most of them so they can bring you the new clients you want. So be sure to delegate all these strategies to your assistant so your video marketing strategies will continue to run on autopilot with no work required from you. That way you can stay focused on what you do best and what you love to do: helping people live their dreams through the exceptional financial planning services you provide.

And now, you've made it almost all the way to the end of this book! Very good job on staying focused and carrying this task through all the way to completion. That is one of the most important factors in achieving success: our ability to complete what we start. So very good work on that!

As you continue to grow and develop in your understanding of marketing, you'll start to use your videos in more sophisticated ways.

Next, I'm going to touch on three of these advanced strategies, and you can test yourself to see if you're already doing these things.

Bonus Strategy #2: Opt In Boxes

If you haven't already added an Opt In Box to your website, now would be a great time to do this. Here's an example of one of my Opt In Boxes:

Figure 18.1 The #1 thing you can do on your website's homepage to generate more new clients is to include an Opt In Box. An Opt In Box will capture contact information from your visitors so you can build a relationship with them over time by continuing to provide valuable content through your email newsletters.

You'll see that my Opt In Box is prominent on the home page of this website: www.JillAddison.com

Most people who visit your website will not become your client immediately. There will be a process of getting to know each other before they become your client. So you must give them a way to get to know you, to stay in touch with you, so that they can grow to know, like and trust you, which often leads to them becoming your client.

One of the best ways to do this is to send them regular email newsletters. So an Opt In Box allows them to sign up for your email newsletter so they can learn more about you and learn more from you over time.

I regularly get new people who I don't even know adding themselves to my email list because I am constantly giving people opportunities to do that. The primary way is through the Opt In Box on my website. But I also post links on my YouTube videos (in the Description box) and in social media inviting people to sign up for my Tips.

Bonus Strategy #3: Maximizing Your Opt In Boxes

If you already have an Opt In Box on your website, give yourself a pat on the back. Good job. Now here are two things you can do to make your Opt In box more effective.

1. Ask yourself, "Would I sign up for this offer? Is it compelling? Am I giving people a good reason to join my email list?" Just saying "Join our newsletter list!" is not going to cut it. You need to hone in on what people really want, and then touch that nerve. A primary principle in marketing is that you must always focus on the question your audience is always asking themselves: "What's In It For Me?" (aka WIIFM). So ask yourself, "What's in it for them if they sign up for my email newsletter list?" We know that most people's primary fear when it comes to finances is running out of money in retirement. So you can touch on that need by including a Call To Action like this: "Get Tips on How to Plan for a More Secure Retirement".

2. Here's the second thing you can do to maximize the effectiveness of your Opt In Box. Sometimes people don't see the Opt In Box right away or they don't take action because it's not screaming for their attention. To get a higher opt in rate, you can use a service like Pop Up Domination. This will make your Opt In Box pop up so it cannot be ignored. Here's an example of what my Pop Up box looks like on my website:

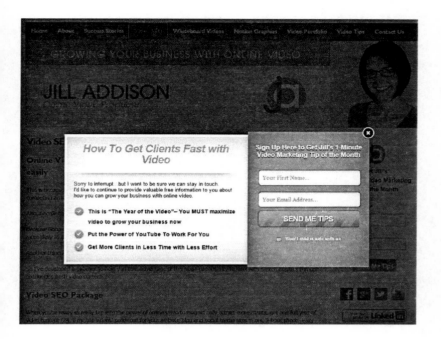

Figure 18.2 To make your Opt In Box even more effective, use a software like Pop Up Domination. When your Opt In Box pops up like this, it becomes impossible to ignore.

I like to set it so this box pops up after someone has arrived on my website and spent about 20 seconds looking around on my site. (Go to www.JillAddison.com to experience this in real time.)

Personally, I don't like it when I arrive on a website and the pop up box pops up immediately. That's not what I came to the site for, so I usually just close it right away. But if I've already been on the site for about 20 seconds, then I'm pretty interested in the content and might be ready to make a bigger commitment to stay in touch by entering my email in a pop up box like this. I've found this timing works well.

So consider having your web person implement a pop up box to increase your opt in rate to join your email newsletter list on your website.

Bonus Strategy #4: Email Autoresponders

As you grow in your marketing skills and understanding, you will probably eventually use autoresponder emails. An autoresponder email sequence is a series of emails that go out when someone takes a specific action.

So for instance, you might want to use your series of videos as an autoresponder email series. You could have an Opt In Box on your website that says, "Get Our 12 Video Tips About How to Plan for a More Secure Retirement". Then whenever anyone signs up, your autoresponder email series will automatically be emailed to them at timed intervals. So for instance, you might set it up so that they get a new email every week for 12 weeks after they sign up.

Even free email newsletter services like Mailchimp offer this advanced functionality, so you can likely use this strategy right now.

Here's the beauty of autoresponders: If Person A signs up in February, they'll get your 12 video series of emails dripped out to them over the next 3 months. If Person B signs up in June, they'll get that same series of emails dripped out to them over the next 3 months. So this means that you can set up an autoresponder series that will deliver all the same content in the same order with the same timing to your new contacts, no matter when they sign up.

This is a fabulous way to use your video content, since it never runs out. Every new person who signs up for your 12 video tip series, whether it's this year, or next year or 5 years from now, will get the same series of emails, and you'll keep repurposing your video content over and over in this way. This is extremely time-efficient and cost-efficient for you.

The other great thing about this strategy is that you'll continue to generate more and more Views on your YouTube channel, all without any ongoing work from you. As you get more and more Views, YouTube will see that you have valuable content and start to reward you by sending more and more traffic to your videos. So this strategy is not only a great email marketing strategy, it's also a way to optimize your YouTube channel by generating more and more Views.

To learn how to do this strategy with your email newsletter service, just go to www.YouTube.com and do a search for "how to create autoresponders in (your email service)". You should find some helpful video tutorials on YouTube this way, and then you can delegate this strategy to your assistant.

1-Minute Video Marketing Tip of the Month Transcripts

In the first year of my business, I started creating a 1-Minute Video Tip each month that I emailed to the people on my email newsletter list to provide valuable content about how to grow your business with video marketing.

What follows are the transcriptions of my 1-Minute Video Tips to date. I hope these tips inspire you to do something similar to these tips to grow your business.

To make it efficient, I always batch produce these tips. That means that I only sit down in a studio twice a year and I film six tips at a time. This ensures that I stay consistent, and it's a much better use of time than creating these tips each month.

I shoot them all at once, have my editor edit them all at once, and then have my assistant schedule them to drip out through my email marketing, social media and blog all at once. So all this marketing runs for me on autopilot, and it only takes me a few hours every six months to keep it running.

> **If you're not already getting my Tips each month, sign up here:** www.JillAddison.com

> **To watch these video tips on YouTube, visit:**
> www.bit.do/1MinTips

How to Win at the Numbers Game

Thanks for taking one minute of your time to let me connect with you again personally.

Here's my 1-Minute Video Tip for this month:

We all know that people like to buy products and services through people they know and people they like.

So if you could be meeting hundreds of people every week, your business would explode, because it's a numbers game. The more sales opportunities you have, the more you'll sell. But who has time to meet hundreds of people every week?

What if people could virtually "meet" you online—on your website, your social media sites, and through email? What if you could make a personal connection with your prospective customers and clients, 24/7, over and over, with no ongoing effort from you? That's what video enables you to do: to be everywhere at once, selling your services in a compelling, visual, and personal way. Video is the next best thing to meeting someone in person. And you can't be everywhere at once. So why not let video do the work for you?

Stay tuned for next month's tip, when I'll share with you 5 Ways to Get Your Online Video Seen. See you then!

1-Minute Video Marketing Tip of the Month #2

5 Ways to Get your Online Video Seen

Ok, so you have a video, now where should you put it so people will watch it? Here are some ideas.

YouTube—Create a personalized YouTube channel. YouTube is the second biggest search engine in the world, so be sure to optimize it for search.

Your Website—Put your video in the upper left corner of your home page. This is where videos are positioned on most video sharing sites, so it signals to viewers that this is video content they want to watch, not advertisements they don't.

Social Media—post a link to your video in the Profile or Info section of your Facebook or LinkedIn account. Also, post the link as a status update and embed the video there.

Email a link to your email newsletter list. Ask them to forward it to five friends and offer them a referral bonus if you do business with their friends.

Me—let me promote the video I create for you on my website, social media sites, and in presentations and trade shows.

Stay tuned for next month's tip, when I'll share with you how you can beat out your competitors by being an early adopter of online video.

1-Minute Video Marketing Tip of the Month #3

The Hidden Power of Pulling the Trigger NOW

A professor at USC studied all of the economic downturns since 1900.

He looked at companies that cut their spending on marketing and advertising and those that maintained or increased their spending on marketing and advertising.

Those that increased their spending not only gained market share, revenue, sales and profits far beyond what they spent, but the beneficial effects lasted for years afterwards, sometimes for decades! Kellogg's, for example, overtook Post Cereal in the 1930s in this way and Post is still trying to catch up. According to a study at a well-known business school, Online Marketing will be the fastest growing segment of Marketing budgets over the next 12 months.

Those who are early adopters of these new technologies will position themselves to flourish in the short term, and also will gain an edge over their competition that could last for years or even decades.

Stay tuned for next month's tip, when I'll share with you 3 Secrets of Why Online Video Works to Grow your Business.

3 Secrets of Why Online Video Works to Grow Your Business

Video on your website increases engagement with your visitors and extends the amount of time they'll spend on your website. On websites with video, the average visitor stays for 6 minutes. On Websites without video, the average visitor stays for 57 seconds.

Video engages people like this because it involves more of their senses.

For instance, a man was traveling through Africa. There was a woman selling oranges, but instead of sitting on the side of the street, she cut up her oranges and said, "Try this orange, smell it, taste it, look how beautiful it is." He tasted the orange and he was hooked. Video is like this too—it helps sell through involving more of the senses. It's sight, sound, music, human voices, all of these things engage us.

Video also increases engagement through telling a story. For instance, an ad for jam doesn't say, "This is jam you can put on your bread." It says, "This jam was made from a recipe passed down for generations. It all began in the misty forests of Bavaria where they grow the sweetest fruits in the world." Much more appealing, don't you think? Videos are a great medium for story-telling, since they're visual and emotional.

Stay tuned for next month's tip when I'll share with you how emotion affects buying decisions, and how video helps you capture emotion.

The Heart of the Matter, and How It Impacts Your Bottom Line

Video engages consumers so well because it's personal. It's like the difference between reading about someone and meeting them in person. Text on your website is just reading about someone. Video is like meeting you in person. And we all know, people like to buy from people they know. Video helps your prospective customers feel like they know you personally.

Because of the personal nature of video, it's particularly good at involving people emotionally. Recent consumer surveys show that, in most cases, 20% of the decision to make a purchase is logical and 80% is emotional.

The single biggest motivator in buying is not the facts, it's emotional response. Humans buy when they feel comfortable, when they feel they can trust you, and when the process feels natural and reassuring. Video can tap into that and involve your prospective client's emotions, helping them feel good about buying from you.

Stay tuned for next month's tip, when I share with you Why Search Engines Love Video.

Why Search Engines Love Video

Because online video is so popular, it's becoming not only a communication tool, but also a search engine optimization tool. Now search engines are prioritizing video in their search criteria, so if you have video on your website or your blog, your website or blog will show up higher in Google rankings.

That's because search engines mimic consumer behavior. Whatever is important to Google searchers is important to Google. Since 60% of online searches are now for video, Google is falling in stride with that preference by prioritizing video in their searches.

Another way Google is focusing on video is by providing a place in your local search profile to upload your own videos. If you don't know what local search is, you're missing a quick and affordable way to get to the top of Google searches for your area. Here's a resource for you to maximize your Google Local Search.

Stay tuned for next month's 1 Minute Video Marketing Tip. See you then.

1-Minute Video Marketing Tip of the Month #7

Why Search Engines Love Video-Part 2

Last month I talked about Why Search Engines Love Video, but this month I want to get more specific, because this represents a huge opportunity for your business.

Here's how it works: when you have a website, you're competing against thousands or even hundreds of thousands of other websites to get that coveted page one of Google. But not that many people have online videos yet that are properly optimized for search, so it's a wide open field. You might only be competing against a handful of other videos that are correctly optimized with your keyword phrases. What this means for your business is that online video can offer a secret back door to get on the first page of Google. So don't wait. This door of opportunity will close as more people recognize that video is key being found online.

Stay tuned for next month's tip, when I'll talk about how social media is starting to integrate with email marketing. In the meantime, check out my logo (point to side).

If Email Marketing and Social Media had a Love Child...

This month I'd like to share with you how you can leverage your email marketing with social media strategies that expand the reach of this traditional marketing strategy exponentially.

You might have noticed that these Video Tips come in an email that has social media buttons across the top. You can just click on those buttons to share my content with everyone in your Facebook, LinkedIn or Twitter networks. If you find this content helpful today, I hope you'll share it.

Secondly, now I can share my email newsletter content with my networks on Facebook, LinkedIn and Twitter easily through Constant Contact's new sharing features.

This enables me expand my email marketing campaign to hundreds or even thousands more people with just a few mouse clicks. It also makes it easy for those people to sign up to receive future Video Tip emails from me.

Stay tuned for next month's tip when we'll talk about how you can leverage social media buttons on your website as well.

Let other people promote your website with just one click

Happy New Year!

Last month we talked about how you can leverage your email marketing with social media strategies that expand the reach of this traditional marketing strategy exponentially.

This month we'll talk about how you can leverage your website with the same kind of social media Share buttons.

Now, it's possible for people who like your website to share it with everyone in their social media networks with just one click of their mouse. After I learned how to add Facebook buttons to my website, I shared the fact that I just learned how to do that on all my social media sites, with a link to my website so others could see how this strategy works.

This is just one more example of how you can maximize the reach of traditional marketing platforms like your website or email marketing with social media strategies.

Stay tuned for next month's tip when we'll talk about how to combine the power of email marketing with the popularity of online video.

How to Amp Up Your Email Marketing with Online Video

For all the popularity of social media, email is still the #1 way that most people use the internet. Ninety-one percent of all internet users use email, and most of them check it daily.

So how can you combine the power of email marketing with the popularity of online video? You're looking at it. My average video email newsletter gets a 35% open rate.

That's compared to the average email newsletter open rate of 10-12%.

This means that video email newsletters can get you in front of 3 times as many people as a regular email newsletter. I'd love to help you get set up with a video email newsletter just like this one to connect with your prospective clients, so let me know if I can help.

Stay tuned for next month's tip when I'll tell you about how you can incorporate video into your daily email communications with no additional ongoing effort from you. See you then.

1-Minute Video Marketing Tip of the Month #11

How to Watch Video from Within Your Inbox

This month I want to tell you about a nifty way to you can incorporate online video into your marketing every day.

It's very effective, and after the initial set up, it takes absolutely no ongoing effort from you.

Web-based email systems like gmail and yahoo have made it possible to paste a link from YouTube into an email, and then your recipient can actually view the video from within the email. They don't have to even click through to another page. I include a link to my video in my automatic signature, so every single person I send an email to has a quick and easy way to watch my video and understand my services better. They can also easily forward it to others they know who may benefit from my services as well.

To make sure your video plays from within email, be sure to copy the link from the My Videos page of YouTube, not the Channel page.

Stay tuned for next month's tip when we'll talk about How Video Unlocks the Secret of Sales. See you then.

Success Story for Increasing Sales

Last year I gave a talk about How To Grow Your Business Through Online Video.

A few months later I heard back from someone who listened to the talk, and then revamped their website to include video. After less than a month, they already had people commenting that they understood the products so much better, and their sales went up.

This is the key to sales. People need to understand what you're offering and why it will help them. Video is able to communicate about your products and services in a way that text just can't.

For those selling products, video makes demonstration of the product possible.

For those selling services, video helps you make the personal connection you need to sell yourself.

Have a great month, and I'll see you next month for the next 1 Minute Video Marketing.

How to Spot an Opportunity on Google

Here's a simple exercise I'd like you to try right now.

Type into Google the top search words that you'd like to be found with on search engines. See if there's any video results that pops up on the first page. If there's not, there's a good chance that you could get on Google Page 1 by creating a video and properly optimizing it for search.

Google wants to return at least one video result on Page One for every search term. So if you have a video optimized for your keywords, that Page 1 spot could be yours.

Online video is a wide open playing field right now, so don't wait. If you need help with creating or optimizing your video for search, just let me know.

Stay tuned for next month's tip when we'll talk about what you should say in your video.

1-Minute Video Marketing Tip of the Month #14

What to Say in Your Video

A lot of people tell me, "I just don't know what I would say in a video."

Here's the most important thing to communicate: your Competitive Advantage. What makes you special? How are you different than your competitors? Why do people love you and want to work with you?

This differentiation should be at the heart of your message when you produce that one polished, professional video for your website.

I'm an expert in understanding why people love you, so if you need some help with this, give me a shout.

And stay tuned for next month's tip when we'll talk about How to Turn an Objection into a Reason to Buy. See you then.

1-Minute Video Marketing Tip of the Month #15

How to Turn an Objection into a Reason to Buy

Objections are the number one reason people don't buy. They have some objection to buying.

So here's a novel approach. Why not start with their objection? It's what's in the forefront of their mind anyway, and they can't really listen to anything you're saying until you overcome that objection.

Here's an example. Maybe your prospective client thinks your services take too long. You can turn this into a reason to buy by pointing out that quality takes time. Your services do take longer, because you're committed to a quality product that will only happen if you take the time to make it just right. Think through the objections you've heard from your prospective clients, and then think about how you can make that objection a reason to buy. Then lead with that in your sales conversation.

Stay tuned for next month's tip when we'll talk about The One Essential Question you should ask yourself before scripting your next marketing piece.

The One Question You Should Ask Yourself Before Scripting Your Next Marketing Piece

Here's the one question you should ask yourself before scripting your next marketing communication piece. Ready?

"What is the one thing that people need to know about you to do business with you?"

I asked a dentist this question for a recent video and he surprised me with a piece of information that no other question had surfaced. He said when he was a kid, he had a phobia of the dentist. Jackpot. The biggest obstacle his prospective clients had to coming to the dentist was fear. So that gave us a perfect way to connect emotionally with them.

Check out his 1-Minute video to see how it worked. ...Go on, seriously, click it.

Why Google Search is Becoming Irrelevant

For most of the last decade, getting on Page 1 of Google has been the holy grail of online marketing. But that's changing. Social Search is steadily taking over as the most powerful and effective search tool online.

When your prospective clients hear about you from a Friend on Facebook, someone they're following on Twitter, or a Connection on LinkedIn, that recommendation carries more weight than what an impersonal algorithm spits out on Google.

One company tracking their online referrers found that their Facebook page, with fewer than 500 active friends, referred 12 times the number of visitors as Google did over the last year.

So if you're not in the Social Media game yet, it's time. Stay tuned for next month's tip when we'll talk about how an accountant revolutionized his company's social media strategy.

1-Minute Video Marketing Tip of the Month #18

One Simple Tweak to Build Stronger Relationships with your Current Customers

Recently I heard about a company where a genius idea for creating good will with current customers came from the accounting department.

An employee noticed that the company sent out dozens of invoices each week, and most of the page was blank. Why not use that blank space to engage customers? So they began printing links to white papers, social media sites and blog posts in that space, and their response rate skyrocketed.

Instead of being bummed about getting an invoice, their customers felt like they were receiving valuable information every time they were billed.

Stay tuned for next month, when I'll be back with the next 1-Minute Video Marketing Tip of the Month.

New Kind of Video for Women Entrepreneurs

This month I have something totally new to tell you about.

I recently created a new kind of video for women entrepreneurs. It's an online show called The Bloom Channel, Where Successful Women Entrepreneurs Share Their Stories. This show gives women who have successfully started and grown their own businesses a place to be showcased as experts. It also gives you a way to connect personally with prospective clients in a very natural interview style. You are cordially invited to visit The Bloom Channel at this address. (*point down*) If you'd like to be notified by email every time a new Bloom Interview posts, you can sign up here. Or you can Get It How You Like It on these major social media networks. And please don't forget to pass this link on to the successful woman entrepreneur in your life.

At Bloom, we have a plan to lift up women entrepreneurs everywhere. I'd love for you to be part of it. Stay tuned for next month's tip when I'll share some statistics about online video that you need to know about.

5 Statistics About Online Video You Need to Know

When it comes to online video, here are some statistics you should know about.

Mobile internet usage will overtake desktop usage in two years.

There are currently about four thousand types of mobile devices on the market.

Over five hundred million videos are watched on mobile devices every day.

The average person spends over five hours per month watching YouTube videos.

Web video is the fastest growing form of media in the history of the world.

If you're not yet using online video to grow your business, you're missing out on one of the most powerful and affordable marketing tools available today. If you have questions about how this could work for your business, please give me a call. I'd love to answer any questions you have. Stay tuned for next month's tip when we'll talk about the pros and cons of homemade video versus professional video.

DIY video vs Professional Video–the Pros and Cons

In thinking about using online video to grow your business, you may be asking yourself whether you should just do it yourself or hire a professional.

Here are some pros and cons for both.

Homemade video can be the perfect solution if you want to create lots and lots of disposable content, like if you're going to post something every week. In that case, people don't expect it all to be professional quality. And sometimes the homemade look can make you seem more authentic, and that can be a good thing.

However, it could also make you look unprofessional and like you don't care enough about your business to invest in it. Professional video will of course give you a more professional image. And professional scripting can make sure that your video hits the mark and produces the results you want. I've produced over one hundred online videos for small business owners in San Diego, and I'd love to do one for you too. Stay tuned for next month's tip when we'll talk about the best way to host your video on your website.

YouTube Vs. Your Website–which is better for your video?

Let's say you already have videos for your business. Should you host them on YouTube or your website? Here are pros and cons for both.

The short answer is, your videos should appear in both places.

YouTube is the second biggest search engine in the world, so you need to be there. And online video will make your *website* stickier; visitors will engage and stay on your page longer with video. The videos on your website can be hosted on your own website, or embedded on your website from YouTube. The advantage of using a YouTube Embed Code is that all the views on your website video will then count as views on your YouTube Channel. That will help you rank higher in YouTube searches. The advantage of hosting your videos on your own website is that then your own website will get the google credit for video and will rank higher with search engines. If you're confused, just call me.

And stay tuned for next month's tip when we'll talk about how to supercharge your YouTube video to get higher search engine rankings

How to Make the Most of your YouTube Video for Search Engines

How can you make sure that your YouTube video ranks as high as possible with search engines? Here are some ideas.

Maximize every way that people can interact with your video. Email your friends, clients, everyone on your email newsletter list and ask them to Like, Share, Favorite, Comment on and most importantly View your video.

The more interaction you have on your video, the higher you'll get in the search engine rankings. And don't forget to optimize your video for humans too. Include a hyperlink to your website so real human beings can find your website from your YouTube Channel. Make sure you begin the website with http:// — this will make it a clickable link. Also, remember to include your phone number. These two pieces of information should be the first thing in your Description box, so visitors can easily contact you from your YouTube Channel.

If I can help you create a video for YouTube, give me a shout. Stay tuned for next month's tip when we'll talk about what we can learn from a room full of kindergarteners.

What We Can Learn from a Room full of Kindergarteners

Recently I was in a room full of kindergarteners. As you might imagine, it was loud.

There was a woman in the front trying to get their attention, but it wasn't working too well. But then she started to tell a story, and suddenly all these fidgety little kids were very quiet and still.

This is a testament to the power of story. From the time we're little children until we're old, we're all captivated by stories.

You can captivate your potential clients with the power of your story. Let them hear it straight from you in a video, and you'll find that suddenly, they're listening to you and feeling connected to your story.

I'd love to help you tell your story, so please get in touch if I can help. And stay tuned for next month's 1-Minute Video Marketing Tip of the Month.

Google Can Hear You

Brace yourself, because this is going to freak you out.

The word on the street is that Google can now hear what your video is saying. There's no way to know for sure what goes on behind the curtain at Google, but it seems clear that now, even the audio in your video is searchable.

What this means for you is that the first few words out of your mouth should include your keywords. Whatever words you want to be found for on Google, include those as close as possible to the beginning of your video script.

Stay tuned for my next Tip when we'll talk about a new strategy to dominate search engine results through video.

1-Minute Video Marketing Tip of the Month #26

How to Use Video to Dominate Search Engine Results

Here's a new strategy for how to use video to be found by search engines. It's called content flood.

Basically you create a new video each week, upload it to YouTube, and make sure your keywords are in the Title, Description and Tags area on YouTube.

It doesn't have to be a masterpiece. You can even just use PowerPoint to create a simple slideshow, then capture that slideshow with Camtasia or Screenflow or another screencast software.

The key is consistency. If you apply this new strategy consistently, you can dominate the search engines for your keywords, using video.

Stay tuned for my next tip when you'll get another free sample of the content of my Do It Yourself Video Package. We'll talk about one simple key that will improve your video scripts 100%.

1-Minute Video Marketing Tip of the Month #27

How to Write Video Scripts

Here's a quick free sample from my Do It Yourself Video Package to help you improve your scripts today:

(www.DIYVideoPackage.com)

Use short words and short sentences. Writing a script is very different than writing a letter. Hearing something is a lot different than reading it. See how easy it is to listen to these short sentences? But if I start speaking in long, convoluted sentences, with complicated words and sentence structure, even if all the information is good and would work if you were reading it, it can become cumbersome and people can get so lost that they forget where this sentence started and they certainly don't know where they're supposed to end up. That was a long sentence. It didn't work so well for video. So the key is, write the way you speak, not the way you write."

Stay tuned for my next tip, when we'll talk about how you can coach your testimonials to get the best video testimonials possible.

How to Get Great Testimonial Videos

Here's another free sample from the Do It Yourself Video Package. In this Tip we're talking about how to coach your testimonials to get the best testimonial videos possible.

If you're planning to incorporate testimonials in your script, write down what you would ideally like them to say about you. When you film them, you can read them your rough draft so they have an idea of the kind of thing you'd like them to say. Then let them put it in their own words. This will help your testimonials communicate about targeted benefits you offer your clients. They need a little direction, so be sure to communicate about this with them.

Stay tuned for my next tip, when we'll talk about the #1 thing you can do in your video to get the response you want.

How to Get the Response You Want from Your Videos

Here's another free sample from the Do It Yourself Video Package. This time we're talking about the #1 thing you can do in your video to get the response you want.

Here's one of the most important keys for getting the response you want to your video: Ask for it. This is called a CTA, a Call to Action. At the end of your video, what action do you want your prospective client to take? Do you want them to visit your website? Call you? Email you? Give you their email address? Subscribe to your YouTube Channel? Like your Facebook page? Whatever the step is that you want them to take, spell it out for them. You could say something like "I'd love to talk with you about how I could help (fill in the blank with your service or product). Please give me a call and we'll get started right away." Then list your phone number, website, or whatever method you want them to use to contact you. More on that in the editing section.

Stay tuned for next month's tip, when we'll talk about the one aspect of your videos that can make or break their effectiveness.

1-Minute Video Marketing Tip of the Month #30

The One Thing that Can Make Or Break your Video

In this free sample from the Do It Yourself Video Package, you'll learn about the one aspect of your videos that can make or break their effectiveness: audio.

For audio, the best way to ensure good audio is to buy a camera that has an external mic jack. Then get a lavalier microphone you can clip on to your shirt to capture clean audio. The closer the mic is to your mouth, the better audio you'll get. With a lavalier mic, you want to attach it between the second and third button, and make sure it's not being rubbed or jostled by any fabric. (zoom in on my lav) The mic can pick up those little sounds. The best fabrics to wear are wool or cotton. The noisiest fabrics are synthetic and silk, so try to avoid those.

Thanks for watching, and stay tuned for next month's 1 Minute Video Marketing Tip of the Month.

The Most Strategic (and Easiest!) Way Get on Google Page One

This month, I'm going to share with you how I got my own website (point to website) to Google Page 1 for my most competitive keyword phrase: San Diego Video Production.

I did it with my new Video SEO Package strategy.

Basically, I took all these 1-Minute Tips that I've been sending out for the last 3 years and scheduled them to release as blog posts on my website every few days, using YouTube Embed codes.

After a couple months, voila, I was on Google Page 1. And this is the only strategy I was using to do this, so it was 100% because of my Video SEO Package that I got these results.

I'd love to help you get these results too, so please check out my Video SEO Package at www.JillAddison.com/video-seo.

Please get in touch and let me help you get to Google Page 1 using Video.

Stay tuned for my next tip on how People Make Buying Decisions. It's not what you think. Oh, and be sure to subscribe to this YouTube Channel to get more ideas for how you can grow your business with online video.

How People Make Buying Decisions–It's Not What You Think!

To understand how people make buying decisions, you need to understand how our brains are made.

Our outer brain, called the Neocortex–is responsible for rational/analytical thought and language. The inner part of brain, called the Limbic brain, is responsible for feelings, like trust and loyalty. It's responsible for all human decision making and behavior, and it has no capacity for language.

When we communicate from the outside in, our prospective clients can understand all the information, the features and benefits of what we're offering, but it doesn't drive behavior.

However, when we communicate inside out, talking directly to the part of brain that controls decision-making, then people take action and later rationalize those decisions based on facts and information. There are so many applications here for how you're communicating about your business.

People will buy from you not because of what you provide, but because of how you or your product made them feel. I'd love to help you script your videos so you're sure you're talking to the right part of people's brains. Give me a call if I can help. And stay tuned for my next tip on how you can make a thousand dollars an hour or more.

How to Make $1000/hour or More

One of the hottest ways to leverage your income today is through webinars.

Most webinars include a video component, either seeing the speaker on video, or usually seeing a PowerPoint as you hear their voice. So it's a powerful combination of using online video and making a live personal connection online.

In webinars you can provide a lot of free valuable information about your area of expertise, and that will entice people to spend an hour or more with you online. Then they'll feel comfortable that you have lots of great information to share. At that point, you can offer them a chance to take it to the next level by buying your information product. Maybe it's an e-book or a series of online videos to train them in your area. I have personally made a thousand dollars in one hour just from selling my Do It Yourself Video Package on a webinar, and I know there's potential to make way more than a thousand an hour doing this. If you'd like to create your own information product to sell on webinars, I'd love to help you script and shoot your video content, so let me know if I can help.

Stay tuned for my next tip on What to Put in the Background of your Video.

What to Put in the Background of your Videos

In this tip, I'm answering one of the most frequently asked questions about video: What Should I Put in the Background. Here's a clip from my Do It Yourself Video Package with some ideas:

(DIY What to Put In Background footage)

Stay tuned for my next tip on the Easiest Lighting Trick for Video, and it's free.

And be sure to subscribe to this YouTube Channel to get more ideas for how you can grow your business with online video.

Easiest Lighting Trick for Video (and it's Free!)

In this tip, I'm sharing a free and easy way to light your video for beautiful results. Here's a clip from Do It Yourself Video Package to show you how:

(DIY Easy Lighting Trick footage)

Stay tuned for my next tip on how to open the door to your client's heart. I bet you don't know what it is.

The Door to Your Client's Heart,
Bet You Don't Know What It Is

The door to your client's heart when they're online is not what you might think. It's your keywords. Keywords are the words people type into google, YouTube and other search engines to find what they want.

By optimizing your videos with the right keywords, you ensure that you are helping people find the exact content they're searching for.

If don't know your Top 10 Keywords, give me a call and I'll help you find them with my proven keyword research process. Or if you need help optimizing your video for your keywords, I'm here to help with that too.

Stay tuned for my next 1-Minute Video Marketing Tip.

How to Make Your Business Matter

Everyone searches for meaning. A lot of people search for meaning in work. People also look for meaning through helping other people.

I've found a way to combine my work with helping others through my Matching Fund for African Women Entrepreneurs.

I've been to Africa twice and I loved it. And I love the new trend of helping African women start their own businesses with microloans.

A loan of even $50 is enough to get her business off the ground and help her feed and educate her children.

So, I invite each of my clients to give an additional 25 dollars, then I match that 25 dollars, and together we provide one microloan for a woman African entrepreneur, every time I get a new client.

It makes me feel good, it makes my clients feel good, and I know it's helping dozens of women entrepreneurs in Africa feel very good.

I hope you'll create a matching fund to invite your clients to help you fund your favorite charity.

Whiteboard Animated Videos-The Newest Trend in Video

Whiteboard animated videos. Everyone loves them. And they're a great way to get a large amount of video for your business without actually having to get on camera.

It takes very little work from you to pull this off. And with all the changes to Google's algorithm, it's more important than ever to have a large volume of engaging videos that you can put on your YouTube Channel, drip out on your website's blog, and post to your social media sites.

But do you have the time to create all this video content yourself? No. That's why you need my Whiteboard Animated Video Package. You can get two new whiteboard animated videos every month for a low monthly rate. And that's going to make you feel like doing the happy dance.

Check out all the details at Jill Addison dot com, just click on Whiteboard Animations. I hope I can help you get found on search engines by creating a large volume of engaging videos for your business.

2 Tools to Revolutionize Your Business

If you're looking to save time in your business, I have two great resources I want to share with you today. oDesk and Dropbox.

Odesk is a website where you can find sub-contractors from around the world to outsource to. I've hired web developers, virtual assistants, and video editors on the site, and it's been amazing what's it's done for my business. When I'm outsourcing many of these time-consuming tasks, it frees me up to generate more business and handle more business, without feeling overworked or overwhelmed. I highly recommend oDesk as a source for affordable sub-contractors.

Another tool I've found very helpful in working with outsourced talent around the world is Dropbox. Dropbox enables you to share files, even big video files. I just upload the files I want my outsourced talent to work on to their Dropbox folder, and they download it on their end. So easy. You can get 2 gigs of storage space for free, or 100 gigs for about $10 a month. I hope you'll take the plunge to start outsourcing big chunks of your business. You're going to be amazed at how it helps your business grow.

More is More?

You've heard the saying, "Less is more". But when it comes to your video marketing, "More is more."

The more video content you have, the better results you'll get. Google loves video right now. When you are consistently putting new, fresh video content on your website, Google will start to rank you higher in search engine results. I started dripping out these 1-Minute Video Marketing Tips to my blog every 3 days or so, and I watched my website climb to Google Page 1 for some of my most competitive keyword phrases. You can also upload your videos to YouTube.

YouTube is the second biggest search engine in the world, and it's owned by Google. Google wants to return at least one video result on Page One of each and every search, so your YouTube videos will help you rank with YouTube and Google. And lastly, you can repurpose your videos a third time by dripping them out to your social media sites. I recommend using a free aggregator like Hootsuite to schedule all your social media posts at once. This is a big time saver, and it's something you can outsource to save even more time. If you're wondering how you'll ever find the time to create the volume of videos you need for your business, check out my Packages where you can get 24 short videos without spending a lot of time or money. Click on Video SEO or Whiteboard Animations on my website for more information.

2 Magic Ingredients to Grow Your Business

One of the most important lessons I've learned in my business is the magic of repeat business and recurring revenue.

These two things are what have really made my business take off in the last year. To get more repeat business, I started targeting businesses with bigger budgets. When a company can afford to pay you over and over, that's the start of a beautiful relationship.

To get recurring revenue, I racked my brain for what kind of product I could create that people would pay me for every month. The answer turned out to be simple: monthly videos. So I started offering 2 whiteboard animated videos every month for a low monthly rate. Just offering this package has increased my revenues by 30%, and I sleep better at night because I know where my paycheck is coming from next month.

Ask yourself, what can I do to get more repeat business and recurring revenue. These two things can explode your business like nothing else.

2 Tools for Super Fast and Easy Videos

Here are 2 great tools that will help you use video in a fast and easy way, with great results.

The first tool is Jing. This is a screen capture software. It's like Camtasia's little brother. It's free, and you can make videos up to 5 minutes long. Then Jing generates a link for you that you can instantly email to others or post online. It's a great way to make a quick screen capture video and post a link to it easily.

The second tool is the Blue Yeti Microphone. I just got one of these, and it provides great audio for screencast videos or webinars and it's very user friendly. Plus it looks cool and makes you feel like an old time radio star. If you want to do quick screencast videos, these two tools are great ones to have in your back pocket.

1-Minute Video Marketing Tip of the Month #43

The Power of Your Goals in 2014

Last year, I had a goal to double my income. Actually, that's been my goal for the last 3 years. But it finally happened last year. A big part of why it happened was because I finally broke that big annual goal into manageable weekly goals.

Every week, I wrote down my goal on my To Do list for how much video I needed to sell to stay on track for my annual goal. Thank you, Shirley Guiducci, my great accountant who suggested this.

ERA Accounting Services, (point) check 'em out.

Anyway, it was exciting to see myself on track for my goal all year long, and it kept me motivated each week.

What's your goal for this year? How can you break it down to monthly, weekly or even daily goals? When you do this, you'll see yourself manifesting your big goal a little bit each day.

Please post in the Comments section below this video and let me know one of your goals for this year.

The Perfect Way to Get New Clients (So Easy!)

Over the last year, I've been perfecting my "sales funnel" for my whiteboard animated video package.

At first, (Opt Page 1) I had just the classic elements of an Opt In page: a video(Opt Page 2) (actually 2 videos) (Opt Page 3), a benefit driven headline, (Opt Page 4) benefit rich bullet points, (Opt Page 5) testimonials(Opt Page 6), and an opt in form to collect emails. (Opt Page 7)

Then, I added a sequence of autoresponder emails to deliver my "10 Second Tips for Video Marketing Success". This way I build trust and credibility over time by delivering valuable content regularly.

But the thing I'm most excited about is my latest innovation. Now, when people click on my Opt In page to enter their email, (3 field) I ask them for two more crucial pieces of information: their first name and their phone number.

I have it set up so that when someone opts in to my site with this information I receive an email notification that plays this sound. ("tada" wav file). So I celebrate every time I get a new lead from my site, and I pick up the phone and call that lead. Studies show that if your prospect gets a phone call from you within 10 minutes of visiting your site, your chances of converting that visitor to a client increase by 60%. I've already had this happen to me, where before I called they probably wouldn't have become a client, but by the end of the phone call, they said "Sign me up!"

If you're selling a high dollar item using online leads, consider incorporating a phone call into your sales funnel. There's nothing like that personal touch to convert more website visitors into clients. Sign up at JillAddison dot com (forward slash) get (dash) monthly (dash) videos to see my sales funnel in action.

The Perfect Length for Your Video

Here's a question I get asked a lot, "How long should my video be?" The answer to that question is: your video should be as long as it takes to make your point, but short enough to keep your viewer's attention.

The amount of time a viewer will spend watching your video is directly proportionate to how interested they are in your topic.

I've seen video series where each video is 20 minutes long, because the viewers are very interested in the topic and they'll watch that much content. But for promotional videos, assume that your viewer doesn't know yet if they're interested.

Two minutes is a good goal for the length of a promotional video. If you can make your point in less time than that, even better.

To get ideas for your next videos, watch some of my favorite promotional videos here.

Goldilocks and Your Business-The Similarities Are Frightening

You know the story. In Goldilocks the theme was too small, too big, or just right.

In business, there's a lot of value in offering Small Medium and Large packages of your products and services. Offering different sized packages will ensure you can serve different needs for different types of clients.

The more people you serve, the higher your revenue will climb.

This strategy will also help smooth out your revenue. Each month you'll have little bits that add up to a lot from your small packages, plus you'll have big gushes of income all at once from your larger packages.

And you'll find that the same client will be worth double or triple the revenue, because one client will buy 2 or 3 of your packages at a time.

Think about how you can position your products or services to please even the toughest Goldilocks customer with small, medium and large packages.

Check out my small, medium and large packages, at Jill Addison dot com.

Niches and Systems-How this Powerful Combination can Transform Your Business

You've probably heard the saying, "The Riches are in the Niches". It's true. Here's one reason why.

When you choose a niche, you'll start to get a system down for how you deliver value in that niche. Once you have a system, everything gets faster and easier.

When you work your system over and over, you get better and better at it. You become more of an expert.

What's your niche? Write it down in one sentence underneath this video in the Comments section. Test yourself to make sure you really know your niche by condensing it to just one sentence, and then write it below. I'm looking forward to hearing from you!

Go Slow to Go Fast

Sometimes we get going so fast in our business that our activity starts to lose focus and get less effective. That's why we need to go slow to go fast,

One way to do this is to track your time. When you write down what you're doing each day in time chunks, you can ask yourself as you go, "Is this what I should be doing with my time? Or is this something I could delegate? " Focus on the things only you can do, the things you do best and that give you the most energy, then delegate the rest.

You can hire a virtual assistant on oDesk for less than $10/hour. So ask yourself, how much is your time worth? If it's worth more than $10/hour, then you need to delegate more.

At the end of each day, review how you spent your time and ask yourself again, "Did I make the best use of my time today?"

If your answer is no, write down what will be different tomorrow. Stay tuned for my next 1-Minute Video Marketing Tip of the Month.

The Power of Yes and No

Recently, I started noticing my own reaction to the words "Yes" and "No."

For instance, when I received an email message that started with the word "Yes", I immediately felt good, almost like a little happiness was injected into my day.

Conversely, I noticed that when an email message started with the word "No," I immediately felt a little mad. Even if they were just answering a question I asked and the answer happened to be "No." That word just isn't fun to hear. Especially in email, when you can't hear the tone of voice. So I started purposely avoiding the word "No" in my email communication. Even if my answer was "No," I would find other ways to say it besides starting an email message with the word "No." And I looked for every opportunity to start emails with the word, "Yes" or a substitute, like "Good question," or "Good point."

Now that you've been exposed to this idea, I'd like you to monitor your own reactions to hearing "Yes" or "No," especially in email communications. Then comment on this video to let me know if I'm just crazy, or if everyone likes to hear "Yes" more than "No." Don't forget to leave your comment right below this video. And don't start it with the word "No."

How to Watch Videos Faster

Sometimes people say they would rather read than watch a video, because they can read faster than they can watch video.

But here's a little trick to make watching videos faster too.

You can actually speed up video playback. You can opt in to the experimental HTML5 video playback on YouTube at youtube.com/html5.

Just press the button that says "Request the HTML5 Player" and you'll be instantly set up for free. Then when you watch videos on YouTube, you can just click the gear icon, and sometimes YouTube will give you this option to either slow down or speed up playback.

You'll see that you can speed up the video by 1.5 times or you can even double the speed of playback. When you watch videos faster, you can get through more content in a shorter amount of time. It can also increase comprehension and retention, since you're more focused. Please leave a comment below now if you found this tip helpful.

1-Minute Video Marketing Tip of the Month #51

Case Study-How One Small Business Owner Exploded His Biz with Online Video

Recently I heard about a case study that was so cool I just have to share it with you.

Jason is a small business owner. Business was a little slow, so he thought he'd work on some marketing. He started making videos to answer Frequently Asked Questions he got asked in his business, and he displayed those videos on his blog. Then something incredible happened.

He noticed that when someone watched at least 30 of his videos online before they called him, his closing ratio went from 10% to 80%. These videos made his business tremendously more profitable. They also made it way easier to get new clients with much less work.

To find out how you could get a series of videos about the Frequently Asked Questions you get asked in your business. Check out our Video SEO Package, or our Whiteboard Video Package. Just click the links below.

The First Video You Need to Create For Your Business

If you haven't gotten on the band wagon yet with using online video to grow your business, this tip will help you get started.

The first videos I recommend you create are testimonial videos.

This means you ask your clients to get on camera to share a positive story about how your product or service helped them.

This is some of the most powerful video content you can create. When a prospective client watches your testimonial videos, it will actually have the same effect as a word of mouth referral.

They'll feel like they know the person speaking on the video and they'll believe that person's story about you. The other reason this is the best place to start is because it's super easy. You can even shoot your testimonial videos with your smart phone.

The fact that it will look amateur can actually make your videos seem more authentic and believable. So you have no excuse not to get started with this marketing strategy right away. Stay tuned for my next tip to see some examples of how to use testimonial videos to grow your business.

1-Minute Video Marketing Tip of the Month #53

How to Use Testimonial Videos to Grow Your Business – Part 1

As I promised in my last tip, this tip features an example of how to use testimonial videos to grow your business. Take a look.

(footage from www.DIYVideoPackage.com)

Stay tuned for my next Tip, when I'll show you another approach for how to use testimonial videos to attract new clients.

How to Use Testimonial Videos to Grow Your Business – Part 2

In my last tip, I showed you an example of how to use testimonial videos to grow your business. That video featured statistics and numbers that showed business growth.

For this tip, I'm going to show you a testimonial that uses a different approach: storytelling. Both are valuable marketing techniques, so watch this.

(Testimonial example footage)

Stay tuned for my next 1-Minute Video Marketing Tip.

Your Niche + YouTube = Success

One of the most important assets you can have in your business is a clearly defined niche.

Who do you serve?

When you get super clear about this, it makes everything easier.

Having a niche translates into success on YouTube as well.

When you have a YouTube Channel that's all about one thing, then everything builds on everything else.

You'll get people watching not just one video, but 10 or 20 videos because all your videos relate to what they're interested in.

And you'll get more subscribers to your channel because they know they'll be interested in all your future content too.

Then, YouTube creates a snowball effect.

It's like the bigger your YouTube Channel viewership gets, the more gravitational pull it has. You'll just keep attracting more and more Views.

To build a big, powerful YouTube channel quickly, make sure you have a clearly defined niche.

Thinking 2 Steps Ahead

Sometimes the next step in your business is actually about the step after that.

Here's a little story from my own business to illustrate what I mean.

A few months ago I finally signed up for Infusionsoft. Infusionsoft is a software program for small business. It's a great tool to automate your processes so you can scale your business bigger. I had been thinking about getting Infusionsoft for a few years. But after I finally pulled the trigger, that opened the door for another opportunity I had been thinking about for a while. I decided to finally buy an email list that enabled me to market directly to hundreds of thousands of financial advisors. I never would have even considered buying such a big list, unless I had taken the step before that, which was to automate my business to the point that I could actually handle a huge amount of new business all at once.

So if there's a next step in your business that you've been thinking about taking for a while, remember this: after you take that step, doors will open that are closed until you take that step.

Write in the comments below this video what next step you've been thinking about taking in your business. Then ask yourself, what might come next after that? You never know until you try.

1-Minute Video Marketing Tip of the Month #57

Pros & Cons of Talking Head vs. Whiteboard Videos

People often ask me which is better: whiteboard videos or talking head videos.

First, definitions. Right now you are watching a Talking Head video. It's my head talking. And this is a whiteboard video. You see that it is hand drawing images about your business.

There are Pros and Cons to both. With a talking head video, you make a personal connection. People feel like they know you when they watch you on video, and people like to do business with people they know, like and trust. But sometimes people are afraid to get on camera. That's when whiteboard videos can be a good option, since you don't have to get on camera. And whiteboard videos are the most engaging type of video. People actually experience a little burst of dopamine, which is the hormone associated with happiness. At the moment they recognize what's being drawn in whiteboard videos, they're delighted. And since people make buying decisions based on emotion, providing this enjoyable educational experience for your prospective clients is very effective.

The best solution is probably to have some of both. This way you keep your marketing fresh, and you get the best of both worlds.

To explore our talking head and whiteboard video packages, visit JillAddison dot com.

How Google+ and YouTube Work Together

Here's how Google Plus and YouTube work together.

You might already know that Google owns both of these social media platforms, which is why they're so integrated.

Here's how to make the most of that integration: You can set up your YouTube account so that when you post to YouTube, it automatically posts to Google Plus too. And when you post on Google Plus with a link to a YouTube video, it will automatically include your status update as a comment on your video in YouTube. This can be a big time saver, and can also really help your search engine results. Google rewards you when you are active on their social media sites, like Google Plus and YouTube.

For instance, YouTube videos can rank in Google search engine results. And Google Plus posts can actually elevate your search engine results for your website when you have your website linked to your Google Plus account. So to streamline your posting and rank higher in search engines, get your YouTube and Google Plus accounts connected.

For more helpful tips like this, subscribe here.

Pattern Interrupt—A Goofy Marketing Strategy

Pattern Interrupt is a marketing strategy where you surprise your viewers or readers with something they don't expect, something that breaks the regular pattern.

That gets their attention, which is the whole point of marketing. There are lots of ways to apply Pattern Interrupt.

For instance, you might remember that one time I did one of these tips with a bright yellow wig on. That was a Pattern Interrupt, and it did get people's attention.

I actually had someone run up to me at a networking event after that and say "I will never forget that." It made an impression.

Another example of a pattern interrupt is that one time I didn't get my tip out on time, so I missed a month.

Later at a networking meeting I had someone comment that they noticed I didn't send out my Tip that month.

I interrupted my regular pattern, and it caught their attention. So every once in a while, shake things up and do something unexpected in your marketing.

And whatever you do, do NOT subscribe this YouTube channel. I mean it, don't you dare subscribe to my YouTube Channel.

How Not To Give Up Too Soon

I've noticed that sometimes business owners and professionals give up too soon when it comes to marketing.

For instance, I've had clients who put one video on their Facebook page, got one Like, and decided the whole thing was a failure.

People, come on. You can't give up so easily. Marketing is just like everything else in life. It takes consistency and patience to make it work.

Your prospective clients will need to see dozens of marketing messages before it even really begins to register with them.

So if you're sending out email newsletters, send more than one. If you're posting on social media, post more than once. And if you're promoting your videos through email newsletters or social media, post more than one.

To find out more about how to get a series of videos for your consistent marketing efforts, visit my website now.

The Next Big Thing in Video Marketing –
Meerkat and Periscope

The next big thing in internet video is live streaming apps.

What these services enable you to do is to shoot video on your phone and broadcast it live to the world in real time.

This service basically makes anyone with a smartphone a video broadcast station.

Just a couple months ago, 2 big players launched their live streaming services: Meerkat and Periscope.

When a new social media platform launches, usually people don't really know what to do with it, so it's like the Wild West. Right now there are mostly a lot of random people filming their own brand of reality TV.

But some people are using it really well, like my favorite band, U2. At their concerts, they're doing a segment where they have someone from the audience get on stage and film them for a live stream on Meerkat. They project the feed onto the screen at the event, and you can see people from all over the world posting comments in real time.

I've also seen businesses filming what amounts to live impromptu webinars or trainings and picking up an audience of several hundred viewers spontaneously. This is possible because the technology is so new and the space isn't crowded yet. It's good for you to know about new innovations in video marketing, but that doesn't necessarily mean you need to get on this band wagon right now.

The best thing you can do is to create a video marketing plan, and then execute on that plan consistently. That's how you'll get real results.

I'd love to help you do that with a series of 24 1-minute videos, either of you on camera, or whiteboard videos. To learn more about each of these services, just click on the links below.

1-Minute Video Marketing Tip of the Month #62

How 1 Law Firm 10X'd their Video Marketing ROI

One of my clients, Alicia Dearn, has gotten great results from the whiteboard videos we created for her law practice.

Here's one story: one of her clients runs a payroll company. He saw her video on social media and shared it. That triggered comments and questions from his clients which led to him hiring her for more services. See how this spreads online?

Her return on investment from just that one client and one video was at least 10 times what she invested in her whole series of videos.

Alicia also told me that her click through rate for video content is five times higher than links to articles. People want to watch video. So she's planning to start incorporating video into all her weekly email newsletters.

She also noticed that more people were engaging with her content on her blog and social media when she posted videos. They were making comments, asking questions, and even emailing her and calling her with questions generated from the videos.

Here's one last way she uses her videos: When people reach out for a consultation, she emails them a video related to their concern before the consultation. This positions her as an expert and triggers deeper thinking so she and her prospective client can talk more seriously about engagement. So not only have her videos helped her get new business through people engaging online with her videos, they also help speed up her new client intake process. Wouldn't you like to have results like that?

Click the link below to find out how you can get a Custom series of whiteboard videos to grow your business. Or, to watch Alicia's whiteboard videos, click on the link below.

Don't Listen to Your Heart When It Comes to Your Marketing

The worst thing you can do in your marketing is to just wait and see what kind of marketing you feel like doing this week.

What if you get busy? What if you don't feel like doing your marketing that week? What if you start worrying that you're "bothering" people again with your marketing messages.

When you leave it up to what you feel like doing each week, that's a recipe for disaster in your marketing.

The best way to handle your marketing is to automate it, to set it and forget it.

That way you never miss a beat.

An example of that is these Tips. I only film these tips twice a year, in batches of 6 tips each. Then I email my assistant one time, and have her schedule them to be emailed out each month, and then I forget about them and they run on autopilot for me. That kind of consistency and planning is a key ingredient you need to get an ROI on your marketing efforts and dollars. Let us help you stay consistent with your video marketing by producing a video series you can use all year long. Click the links below for more information.

How to Attract Your Ideal Client

One of the most important exercises you can do in your business is to get very clear about who your Ideal Client is. Once you know this, many new doors will open to you. You can even create an "avatar," which is a fictional person who embodies the traits of your Ideal Client.

Here's quick glimpse at my avatar:

His name is Bill. He's a Financial Advisor and he wants to take his practice to the next level. He's enthusiastic, a hard worker, realistic, and somewhat savvy about marketing and technology. And this is just quick glimpse of what an ideal client might look like for me. You could also list demographic information like age, where they live, how much money they make, what their hobbies are, and on and on.

Now obviously, not every person you work with will fit your avatar description exactly.

But this exercise gives you a good clear focus for who you're trying to attract, and that will affect every marketing decision you make.

Please take a moment and leave us some details about your Ideal Client in the comments below. Leave your website too, so if your Ideal Client sees himself or herself in what you wrote, they can get in touch with you.

How to Stop Working with People Who Make You Feel Bad

In my last Tip, we talked about how to get very clear about who you want to attract as your ideal client.

In this Tip, we're going to talk about an equally important exercise: getting very clear about who you don't want to work with. It's like a crime profile.

So here's my profile for the opposite of my ideal client:

He's aggressive, rude, and deeply frustrated with marketing in general.

He's unhappy, extremely talkative, he often talks in circles, and I can't get off the phone with him. He's a complainer, he wants immediate results or else, and he's not savvy about marketing or technology.

I have learned that people who share several traits in this profile are not my best clients.

So now when I'm on the phone and I start to notice a new prospect fits this profile, I know it's ok to let it go, because he is just not my Ideal Client.

If you missed my last tip about how to attract your Ideal Client, please click here to watch that video now.

Can You Really Make Meaningful Connections on the Internet?

Sometimes people are skeptical about whether they can really make a significant connection with new prospects on the internet.

The internet has truly changed everything. And if you think that you can't begin significant relationships on the internet, I have just one picture for you.

This is my husband and me on our wedding day. We met on the internet.

The transition from an internet relationship to a real relationship is not as difficult as you might think.

With online dating and with business building, the first contact is often made on the internet, but then there's a phone call and then an in-person meeting, and voilà, it's a real relationship.

So if you're still thinking that your best new client can't be someone you met on the internet, think again.

To learn more about how you can meet your next client on the internet, please click on the link below.

Free Bonus with This Book

As the owner of this book, you are entitled to a free 60-minute Online Video Training Seminar (Value: $295) with Jill Addison.

To claim your spot, visit: www.FAVideoTraining.com

In this Online Video Training Seminar, I personally walk you through the best techniques and strategies to maximize the power of online video to grow your financial advisory practice.

You'll hear case studies you can't hear anywhere else, and glean valuable insights for how to replicate those successes in your own business.

You'll Learn:

- How to make people pre-disposed to become your client before you ever meet with them

- How to motivate your clients to refer you to new clients on a regular basis

- How to make your clients LOVE you even more and naturally refer you at a faster and faster rate

- 3 keys to keep your current clients happy

- How to create an online presence that moves people several steps along in your sales process before you ever even talk with them in person

- How to build authority, credibility and celebrity with your video content

- One sneaky little trick that will make it impossible for your clients NOT to refer you

- The one single thing that will make the difference between them referring you or not referring you

- A covert ops way to get testimonial-type credibility that your compliance department will not blink an eye at

- How to strategically get 5-7 bounces out of each video

- How video accelerates every other marketing strategy you have, so it's not just one tool, it's like a super tool that makes every other tool more effective

- How to take your current real life relationships onto the internet, and also how to take your internet relationships into real life relationships

- Why video is working so well, in case you're one of the few who are still skeptical about video

- Our story of how video helps us get calls from people we don't even know, who were referred by people we don't even know, all because of our videos

- And More

This Online Video Training Seminar is free for you as the owner of this book, but be sure to claim your spot right away, because we're not sure how long this training will be available at the link below.

Visit www.FAVideoTraining.com **today to get access to your FREE Bonus 60-Minute Online Video Training Seminar.**

To end this book, I'd like to share with you one of my favorite quotes. This is a quote I've had on my wall for years, and I love it.

> **All our dreams can come true, if we have the courage to pursue them.**
>
> – Walt Disney

This is my hope for you, that all your dreams will come true, and you will have the courage to pursue them.